THE
STACK
AND
TILT
SWING

THE
STACK
AND
TILT
SWING

The Definitive Guide
to the Swing That Is
Remaking Golf

MICHAEL BENNETT and ANDY PLUMMER
with PETER MORRICE

GOTHAM
BOOKS

GOTHAM BOOKS

Published by Penguin Group (USA) Inc.
375 Hudson Street, New York, New York 10014, U.S.A.
Penguin Group (Canada), 90 Eglinton Avenue East, Suite 700, Toronto, Ontario M4P 2Y3, Canada (a division of Pearson Penguin Canada Inc.); Penguin Books Ltd, 80 Strand, London WC2R 0RL, England; Penguin Ireland, 25 St Stephen's Green, Dublin 2, Ireland (a division of Penguin Books Ltd); Penguin Group (Australia), 250 Camberwell Road, Camberwell, Victoria 3124, Australia (a division of Pearson Australia Group Pty Ltd); Penguin Books India Pvt Ltd, 11 Community Centre, Panchsheel Park, New Delhi—110 017, India; Penguin Group (NZ), 67 Apollo Drive, Rosedale, North Shore 0632, New Zealand (a division of Pearson New Zealand Ltd); Penguin Books (South Africa) (Pty) Ltd, 24 Sturdee Avenue, Rosebank, Johannesburg 2196, South Africa

Penguin Books Ltd, Registered Offices: 80 Strand, London WC2R 0RL, England

Published by Gotham Books, a member of Penguin Group (USA) Inc.

First printing, November 2009
10 9 8 7 6 5 4 3 2 1

Copyright © 2009 by AM Golf Associates LLC
All rights reserved

LIBRARY OF CONGRESS CATALOGING-IN-PUBLICATION DATA
Bennett, Michael.
  The stack and tilt swing : the definitive guide to the swing that is remaking golf / Michael Bennett and Andy Plummer with Peter Morrice.
      p. cm.
  ISBN 978-1-592-40447-6 (hardcover)
1. Swing (Golf) I. Plummer, Andy. II. Morrice, Peter. III. Title
  GV979.S9B46 2009
  796.352'3—dc22

                                                                              2009009406

Printed in the United States of America

Photos of Mike Bennett and Andy Plummer from J. D. Cuban. Historical and player photos courtesy *Golf Digest*/Condé Nast Publications

Set in Garth Graphic with Trade Gothic LT Std

Designed by Sabrina Bowers

While the author has made every effort to provide accurate telephone numbers and Internet addresses at the time of publication, neither the publisher nor the author assumes any responsibility for errors, or for changes that occur after publication. Further, the publisher does not have any control over and does not assume any responsibility for author or third-party Web sites or their content.

CONTENTS

FOREWORD

DR. BOB ROTELLA

When you watch a PGA Tour event on television, you might think every player is hitting one perfect shot after another, and that the winner is the one with the hot putter. The truth is, there's a lot of variation in ball-striking on the tour. Players are always trying to find ways to improve their misses, to make their bad shots better. Which is exactly the approach that Andy and Mike take in their teaching.

One thing that makes these guys so well suited for teaching on tour is their earnest dedication to their students. They are as committed to their players as any teacher I've ever seen. You can find them on tour practice ranges every week, every day. That's how passionate they are about what they do—and about the players who have put their trust in them. This is a huge component of the student-teacher relationship.

Andy and Mike also understand the big picture of playing professional golf. They know that to be successful their players have to learn to get the ball in the hole, and that comes from a lot more than swing mechanics. By organizing their students' practice routines and off-weeks, Andy and Mike have helped them separate working on the swing from playing competitive golf. That really impresses me. It shows a level of discipline and understanding that only great teachers have.

My experience as a sport psychologist tells me that the best thing you can do to help a golfer is to give him something he can believe in. Andy and Mike clearly are doing that for their players—and they have a tough task because many of the moves they teach seemingly contradict what is commonly taught today. But their explanations make sense, and then they break out a notebook full of pictures of the great champions demonstrating what they're saying. Suddenly it doesn't seem so radical.

Another thing that strikes me about these two is that their list of tour students has grown by word of mouth alone. I've never heard of them walking up to players and trying to win them over. Their approach is soft-spoken and based on results, not salesmanship. Players see their guys doing well, hitting the ball better, and they want to know more. That's how they've established themselves on tour.

The good news for golfers everywhere is that the work Andy and Mike are doing is starting to trickle down to the golfing public, and this book will accelerate things. In the end, average golfers will be the biggest beneficiaries, because the tour has served as a testing ground for the instruction. If world-class players like Mike Weir and Aaron Baddeley can quickly see positive results, imagine what the swing can do for the weekend player trying to break 90.

Forty years ago, Bob Toski was a revolutionary teacher who changed the way golf was taught; twenty years later, David Leadbetter did the same. Now we have Andy and Mike, and I'd put them in the same conversation. They have joined a small group of teachers who have developed a different approach and seen it catch on. Time will tell if their system earns a place in the history of golf instruction, but for today, it's the hottest method in the game—and now it's literally in your hands.

INTRODUCTION

I f all of the golf instruction books, videos, and lessons for the last hundred years had taught people to keep their weight on the left side and to swing their hands inward, we would have generations of golfers drawing the ball instead of slicing. Golf would be a different game. Instead, most instruction today teaches moves that lead not only to a slice but also to hitting the ground behind the ball, which has inhibited the development of players and the game itself. Golfers are either learning the wrong things, or the right things in the wrong order. Either way, their games are not improving.

Why is this happening? For one, there is no consensus on the basic physics of the game, such as what makes the ball go where it goes. Plus, there is no universal language for golfers to communicate the moves they're making or the shots they're hitting. Consequently, they're forced to use vague clichés, like "I swung too fast" or "I looked up," or other bits of handed-down jargon.

These impediments have made the barrier of entry into golf unnecessarily high. Golfers routinely leave the game out of frustration, lack of direction, regression, or improvement that comes too slowly. Our method is based on geometric principles that are familiar to all, and not on the technique of a random champion golfer or even a generation of successful golfers. It so happens that many players already exhibit the correct swing geometry, whether they know it or not, but modern instruction has not helped them to find it.

This book, then, is not an examination of any particular player's swing but a tool for measuring the difference between a good player and a poor player, and the difference between a good shot and a poor shot. As the old saying goes, golf is a game of inches: We're measuring the inches to make golf instruction understandable and accessible to all players. Remember, geometry and physics are the same for everyone; the anatomy of the individual player's body dictates the actual swing mechanics.

We came to our conclusions and devised the system you're about to learn not just by studying how certain professionals hit the ball, but by applying the rules of science. Then we found evidence of these principles in the game's best players, past and present. But equally important, the principles of Stack & Tilt can be seen on driving ranges and golf courses everywhere. Our decade of research has allowed us to identify a good swing and to recognize all of its pieces. It has been said that the essence of science is classification; through classification we can unlock the pattern for playing golf simply and in an organized way.

As you'll see, much of Stack & Tilt is not new. Elements like straightening the right leg on the backswing, swinging the hands on an inward path, and keeping the weight on the front side can be found in many books that predate us. What *is* new is the establishment of true fundamentals and the explanations of how they function.

⬇ **Straightening the right leg on the backswing is one of the distinctive moves of Stack & Tilt. These players won more than fifty major championships illustrating this concept.**

Swinging the hands well to the inside instead of straight back is a common trait among great ball-strikers.

WHAT IS STACK & TILT?

Put simply, the Stack & Tilt Swing is a mechanically simpler way to hit the ball. The traditional golf swing features a big shift away from the target on the backswing, with the upper body moving behind the ball, and a corresponding shift toward the target on the downswing. The problem with those moves is that as you shift back and through, you must "find the ball" somewhere in the middle. If you don't time the shifts perfectly, you won't make solid contact, which is the first requirement to becoming a proficient golfer.

NO!

The traditional advice to shift the upper body behind the ball leads to inconsistent contact.

Stack & Tilt keeps the body centered over the ball during the backswing and through the shot. There is no guesswork as to where the club will be at impact, no requirement to locate the ball through precise timing. With Stack & Tilt you simply favor your front foot at address and stay there throughout the swing, with no weight ever moving to your back foot. The first fundamental of Stack & Tilt is hitting the ball solidly, and that comes primarily from controlling where your weight is during the swing. If your weight stays in place, contact is predictable; if your weight moves back and forth, it is not.

← **The spine angle must continuously change on the backswing to keep the body centered for consistent contact.**

→ **These great players demonstrate the spine tilting toward the target in varying degrees at the top of the backswing.**

As you'll see, there are many other points of difference between the traditional swing and Stack & Tilt, but this is the most important and most observable one. Swing technique varies greatly, even among the best players, but solid contact is the essential first ingredient. Power, ball control, and other sophisticated traits are common among elite golfers, but nothing outweighs hitting the ball consistently. If you learn to do that, you'll progress quickly.

HOW IT WORKS

We call our method Stack & Tilt because of the way the spine tilts throughout the swing to keep the golfer "stacked," or to keep the upper-body center—the center of the shoulders—in one place during the swing. Our friend PGA Tour player Charlie Wi helped us come up with the name during a practice session a couple of years ago.

↑ **Three key moves of Stack & Tilt:**
Turn the left shoulder down (1),
tilt the spine left (2),
and push the hips through (3).

As we see it, the function of the golf swing is to hit a ball as far as possible, as straight as possible, and as consistently as possible. Stack & Tilt is designed to incorporate these elements. You could devise a swing with the lone goal of hitting the ball farther: The left arm would flex on the backswing to create another lever, the arms would lift off the body to extend the arc, and the golfer would jump off the ground at impact and spin around like a discus thrower. The result might be more power, but the golfer would have no control.

A swing model designed solely to hit the ball straight, with no consideration paid to distance, would also look different—almost like a long chipping stroke. But a golfer chipping the ball around the course would never finish a round. Control without power is even more ineffective than power without control.

Consistency, of course, is the mark of the expert golfer, but consistency without power and control isn't worth much. A golfer who repeatedly slices into the woods or hits the ball 150 yards off every tee is not going to post many good scores. It's the combination of consistency, power, and control that makes a golf swing effective. And that's what we've assembled in Stack & Tilt.

It is also important that the swing be simple enough to repeat. It must not have such a high degree of difficulty under the pretense of being optimum that using it is impractical. Unlike the Olympic gymnast or diver, the golfer must minimize the degree of difficulty so that the swing can be repeated time after time, not just once. The goal, then, is to develop a swing that hits the ball the longest, the straightest, the most often.

We often hear that every golfer is different and, therefore, needs a different swing. We disagree, because the rules of geometry and physics are the same for all golfers, and it is the golfer's job to conform to them and to predict them. The golf ball does not know if the player is fifteen or seventy-five, or fifty pounds overweight. All it knows is what the club tells it at impact.

Impact may be a simple exchange of information from clubface to ball, but the golf swing is a complex motion. What is needed in golf instruction is a standardized system that is simple enough for the beginning golfer but broad enough to allow for increasing levels of sophistication. We need simple metrics and basics from the start that advance in specificity as the golfer's skill level increases. This need has become apparent to us in our careers both as players and teachers.

Often during our years as struggling players we would reconstruct our swings based on the previous bad shot. There was no structural template in place, so every day was a process of trial and error of dramatic changes. We now know that a simple adjustment at address or in the backswing might have sufficed, but not knowing what to do led us to change things that did not need changing and to overlook the offending parts. Every day golfers make these same mistakes.

HOW WE GOT HERE

Playing the mini-tours in the mid-1990s, we became students of golf technique. This was largely out of desperation. We sought out the help of many of golf's most prominent teachers, and at times their advice was exactly what we needed. But periods of improvement were marred by steep declines, which made no sense considering all the time we devoted to practice. There was a lack of order in our understanding; we often didn't know whether to try something new or to go back to something that had worked before, in the hope that it might work again.

During this period we were introduced to *The Golfing Machine,* a somewhat obscure instructional book written in 1969 by Homer Kelley. Kelley was not a competitive golfer or even a teacher until later in life, but his book showed us how science could be applied to golf. The same laws that govern the universe also govern golf. The book used classification as a way of separating the individual elements or components of the swing. This was what we were looking for in our own games: a system of organization. The advice of great teachers like Larry Bartosek, Tom Tomasello, and Mike Bender helped us put into context many of the principles laid out in *The Golfing Machine.*

With the help of another teacher, Mac O'Grady, we started to refine our perspective on the golf swing. His knowledge and guidance encouraged us to dig deeper into the patterns that exist in the game. We examined not only our own swings, but also those of the great players and, ultimately, average golfers. The more we studied historical photos of elite players, the more we saw the patterns develop.

And when we started cataloging the swings of average golfers, the reasons they were average also became clear. Most instructors analyze a golfer's swing only to figure out what that golfer, individually, needs to do. Our systematic analysis of average players has been valuable not only in understanding bad technique but also in helping us see points that apply to even the best players.

During our practice with tour players today we often refer to these pictures of average golfers to make our points. At first the pros don't know how to take this comparison, but before long they're referring to these golfers by name. Over the years we have assembled photo spectrums to exhibit the range of positions for every part of the swing; for example, from the flattest left arm on the backswing to the most upright. We have also created photo catalogs of top players demonstrating the moves we teach. We make up a three-ring binder for each of our players and encourage them to build their own golf book just like ours.

← Cataloging historical photos of elite players has revealed master moves, like the left knee moving forward to start the downswing.

Measuring the process is critical, so we record a lot of swings on video to show a student how a particular change is affecting the flight of the ball. We call this "calibrating with the camera." This is our way of helping the student see what he is actually doing and associate it with a feel. Every golfer is ultimately a feel player. If you're working on the right element or moving in the right direction, you should see results right away. This is what makes the work we do so gratifying: seeing a beginner progress from not being able to hit the ball to flushing shot after shot, or watching a professional go from losing his tour card one year to shooting up the World Ranking the next.

Improvement in golf is available, provided you're ready to rethink what you're doing and embrace an approach based on principles, not quick tips. Mystery and frustration are not inherent qualities of golf, but arise because of the haphazard way the game is learned.

STACK & TILT ON TOUR

In 2005, we videotaped nearly every swing that our friend Steve Elkington took on the range and during practice rounds. We assembled a book for him that tracked his progress using the moves we're about to share with you. In six months, he went from a ranking of 389th in the world to the top 50, finishing a stroke behind Phil Mickelson at the PGA Championship in 2005. That year Steve adopted a strange-looking rehearsal move in his pre-shot routine, tilting his spine dramatically to the left just before he stepped up the ball. It was an exaggeration of the spine tilt we were working on with him, and it got people talking about what we were teaching.

By that time we were already working with Tom Scherrer and Grant Waite, whose improved swings were gaining the attention of fellow pros. Grant introduced us to Dean Wilson, who lost his card after the 2004 season and came to us ready to make changes. Dean became one of our best stories and best friends, working hard on his swing over the next year and eventually winning his first tour event, The International, in 2006. That year Dean finished 22nd on the money list, which got more players asking about Stack & Tilt.

Three more of our tour students, Aaron Baddeley, Will MacKenzie, and Eric Axley, also won for the first time in 2006. By the time Aaron got his second win, at the beginning of 2007, we were both on tour every week, with about a dozen players converted to our model. One of those players was Mike Weir, whose game had slipped since he'd won the Masters in 2004. Mike worked hard to change his form, and in 2007 won in Phoenix and beat Tiger Woods in their singles match at the Presidents Cup. In 2008, Mike finished 14th in earnings on tour, with eight top-10 finishes on the year.

← Since early 2006, Aaron Baddeley has won twice on tour and ranked as high as 17th in the world.

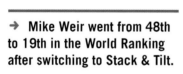

→ Mike Weir went from 48th to 19th in the World Ranking after switching to Stack & Tilt.

People sometimes ask us who best represents Stack & Tilt. Often our answer is Charlie Wi. His transformation is as dramatic as any we've seen. Charlie used to make all of the classic moves thought to produce power and consistency, swinging his hands high in the air and making a big shift behind the ball on the backswing, but he wasn't getting results. Today Charlie is thought of by many players as one of the best ball-strikers on tour, and he exhibits the moves we teach better than any other player. If you want to know what Stack & Tilt should look like, watch Charlie Wi.

While the work we've done with tour players has been very gratifying, our goal is to help as many golfers as possible improve their swings and enjoy the game more. Amateur players have more to gain from Stack & Tilt than tour pros do; they simply have more room for improvement. The pros are already hitting the ball solidly and with plenty of power, but average golfers need everything Stack & Tilt has to offer—above all, its ability to take the mystery out of the game.

At its core Stack & Tilt is a system of organization in which the golf swing is broken down into its basic elements and built up into a sophisticated machine. Cause and effect is the basis for everything we teach. There is no trial and error, no guessing, no reversing course. There is the basic structure of the swing and the added details that make it effective at higher and higher levels. There is a clear starting point and a clear progression, which is what's missing in golf instruction today.

As you go through this book, you'll see comments from tour players on what Stack & Tilt feels like to them at various points in the swing. We're not saying you should copy their feels, but it can only help you to hear how these great players think about the swing—and maybe something they say will click. It's important to remember that feel can be misleading: You have to make sure that what you're feeling corresponds to the correct geometry, which you'll learn over these pages.

There are two ways to use the Stack & Tilt Swing and this book. First, you can learn how and why all the pieces work and start to develop an effective swing from the ground up. That's the first part of the book. Or you can add pieces to your current technique, based on what will make the biggest difference to the flight of the ball. That's the second part of the book. Both approaches will move you toward the same goal: developing a sound, repeatable golf swing.

Throughout the book, we primarily describe the swing from two angles: face-on and downtarget. The face-on view is at a 90-degree angle to the starting line of the shot. Downtarget is from behind the player, looking toward the target. These two angles provide the best pictures of the positions under discussion.

Also, our descriptions apply to right-handed golfers, so we'll often use "left hand" or "right foot" instead of "top hand" or "back foot." We do so because these terms are easier for most golfers to understand. To that same point, we've tried to use plain, simple language whenever possible to get away from the clichés and inaccuracies common in instruction talk.

THE
STACK
AND
TILT
SWING

GOLF'S REAL FUNDAMENTALS

We begin many of our clinics by asking students to name the fundamentals of golf. The answers that come back are invariably the same: grip, stance, posture, alignment, tempo, "square at impact," and a few other bits of traditional golf doctrine. The problem with these so-called fundamentals is that they are not standards exhibited by the best players, which means they are not fundamental at all.

For instance, look at the different grips used by the game's top players. Ben Hogan held the club with his hands basically straight up and down the handle, while Sam Snead's grip was turned dramatically to the right. Jack Nicklaus and Greg Norman rotate their hands slightly to the right. Then consider how the hands are joined. Nicklaus and Tiger Woods use interlocking grips, but most golfers today overlap the hands. No standard exists for the grip among the game's best players. You can go up and down the range at any PGA Tour event and find all sorts of variations in the grip.

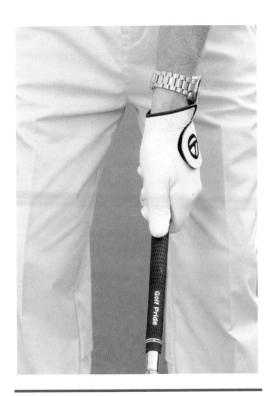 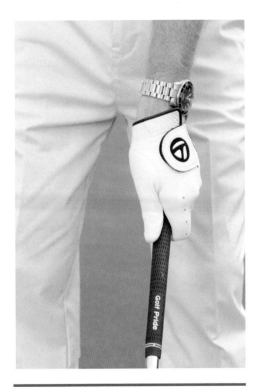

↑ No standard grip exists among the game's best players. Hogan placed the left hand on the club like this.

↑ Snead, Palmer, and many others turned the left hand away from the target.

As for the alignment of the stance, Nicklaus, Lee Trevino, and Fred Couples aim to the left, while Snead and Arnold Palmer had closed stances. How about aiming the club at the target? Practically no golfer aims the club straight. A sniper with a scope gun on a tripod would have trouble aiming at a flagstick 200 yards away, much less a golfer standing to the side of the ball. Elkington aims the club-face 5 to 10 degrees to the right, and Jesper Parnevik aims it to the left. There's no standard in aiming the club or aligning the body.

These golfers have used these variables to hit the ball in a predictable way without using any standard at all. Yet the beginning golfer spends his formative practice time trying to master things that are completely subjective: the perfect grip, the perfect stance, the perfect posture, and so on.

Consider ball position: Bruce Lietzke and Craig Stadler play the ball forward in the stance; Allen Doyle plays it way back. And great players are found everywhere in between. Lietzke's forward ball position helps him play a left-to-right shot, but Trevino puts the ball back and also hits the ball left to right. Again, they've found ways to make it work. How about timing or tempo? Nick Price swings fast, and Couples has a slow tempo. Square at impact? Hardly. Just as few players aim the clubface directly at the target at address, not many have the face pointed at the target at impact, either.

There is no standard in any of these variables, so we prefer to call them "preferences." This has a far-reaching impact, because the fundamentals are the first things a developing player must master to establish the proper progression for learning golf.

We believe a fundamental is something that links all the great players together, something that transcends individual setup and swing positions. It is a characteristic that all great ball-strikers share. What makes it a fundamental is not how they do it, but *that* they do it. That is a critical distinction. The elements that control those basic truths should be the first things a golfer learns.

↑ **Champion golfers also play the ball in different positions.**

↓ **There is no standard for alignment: Some players aim right, some straight, some left.**

THE STACK & TILT FUNDAMENTALS

We teach three fundamentals, to be followed in this order: (1) hitting the ground in the same place every time; (2) having enough power to play the course; and (3) matching the clubface to the swing path to control shot direction. Let's break these down.

The first measurable difference between golfers of different skill levels is the ability to hit the ground in the same place time after time—in other words, the ability to control the low point of the swing. The skilled player can swing the club and hit the ground in the same spot every time. He also hits the ground in front of the ball on every swing, in slightly varying degrees. The less-skilled player hits the ground farther back and with wider dispersion from one shot to the next, nearly in direct proportion to his ability level. The least-skilled player often doesn't hit the ground at all because he pulls his arms apart to keep from hitting behind the ball. When you watch the pros on TV, you'll see that every one of them controls this low point of the swing every time.

We start many of our lessons by scratching a line in the ground and having the student straddle the line as if it were the ball, then try to take divots on the target side of that line. This might seem like a simple exercise, but the inconsistency of the low point begins to surface in just a few swings. This is where the problems start. First, many students don't recognize that the low point is coming behind the ball. Second, once they see the problem, they don't know how to control it. So they revert back to old clichés: "I got quick," "swung too fast," "came over it." Buzz phrases like these have nothing to do with where the club hits the ground, which is the biggest problem with most amateur swings.

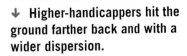

← The expert player can hit the ground in the same spot time after time.

↓ Higher-handicappers hit the ground farther back and with a wider dispersion.

← A trail of divots left by an expert player, and a patch left by a poor player.

When we're working with a golfer, we often ask him to identify where the low point occurred. Then we introduce a few elements that control the low point. The first factor that contributes to the location of the low point is where the body weight is at impact. We measure the weight by locating the swing's two centers—the center of the shoulders (above the sternum) and the center of the hips or pelvis. If the swing's dynamic center, which is the combination of the shoulder and hip centers, is back too far, the swing tends to bottom out behind the ball. If the dynamic center is forward, the swing tends to bottom out in front of the ball.

But you can have the centers forward and still hit too far back, so something else must be involved. The other element is the width of the swing arc as controlled by the angles in the wrists and the forward lean of the shaft as seen from the face-on view. Simply put, the more the shaft leans toward the target, the better the chance that the club will hit the ground farther forward, because the swing radius reaches its full length later. Conversely, the more the shaft leans back, or away from the target, the longer the swing radius gets before it reaches the ball, and the farther behind the ball the club tends to hit the ground.

Many average amateurs, nearly all, violate these principles. They move the centers back too far and are not sophisticated enough to realize how forward and how fast they have to move them to make up for it. Also, they unhinge the wrists, sometimes unconsciously and sometimes consciously if they're under the assumption that they are supposed to roll the wrists through impact to "release the club." These moves put the low point behind the ball and prevent solid contact.

The location of the low point is the first measurable difference between players at different skill levels, so the elements that control the low point are the first things a golfer should learn to recognize and master. The developing golfer must know where the weight is and whether or not the shaft is leaning forward at impact, because together they determine where the club hits the ground. It is our experience that these positions are easy to achieve if they are understood in the beginning and identified when they slip off track.

The second fundamental that is common to good players is generating enough power, in slightly varying degrees, to play the course effectively. The first power element is the path of the hands and the club moving inward—around the body as opposed to upward—on the

The Stack and Tilt Swing

backswing. Moving the hands and club on a circular arc stores potential energy, as compared to moving them straight back over the target line. This dynamic is evident in many sports, perhaps most clearly with field-goal kickers in football. Decades ago, field goals of thirty or forty yards were considered long, because kickers used a straight-line approach. When that technique gave way to the soccer-style method of approaching the ball on an angle, allowing the torso to turn and the leg to swing in an arc, kickers started regularly making fifty-plus-yard field goals.

↑ **These golf legends illustrate a similar hand path, with the hands passing through the body at the base of the right biceps.**

← Golfers who keep the arms in can hit the ball higher and farther.

NO!

→ If the arms move out on the downswing, the swing gets steep and cuts across the ball, causing pulls and slices.

The next factor in creating power is the spine angle changing from flexion (tilting forward) to extension (straightening up) throughout the swing to create additional clubhead speed and launch. This element has eluded golf instruction but lies at the heart of learning to play at a high level. It is this principle that allows the golfer to use the ground as a springboard, much like a long jumper pushing off the runway. Simply put, the golfer on the downswing should slide the hips toward the target and straighten the knees and the forward tilt of the body to catapult the shaft. This extension or elongation of the spine allows the golfer to swing the club into the ball more powerfully.

For clarity, we tell many of our students to raise the belt (straighten the knees) and tuck the butt under the upper body to the finish (elongate the spine). This is an incredibly powerful one-two punch that swings the club through impact at maximum speed. So the sequence is, raise the belt, tuck the butt, extend the spine to the finish. We'll address these moves in detail as we go along.

← **Tiger Woods shows how the spine should move from flexed forward to fully extended during the swing.**

Our third fundamental is developing a predictable pattern of projecting the ball toward the target by controlling the clubface and the swing path. It is here the golfer uses the variables of grip, stance, alignment, and so forth, in a familiar way to hit the ball as intended. The best players have mastered the first two fundamentals—low point and power—so direction control becomes the factor that determines success at the top levels of the game. On tour, where solid contact and power are prerequisites, the ability to control curve and trajectory creates wide gaps among players.

The problem with controlling the curve is that many people do not understand the rules that determine how the ball flies the way it does. In an informal poll we've asked tour players what gives the ball its initial direction, the path of the club or the angle of the clubface. Sixty percent have answered incorrectly, and many golf instruction books over the years have gotten this wrong. It is golf's most basic question. The answer is, it's the clubface that gives the ball its initial direction. Many great players can demonstrate this and other basic principles, but they cannot explain them. That's where the problem lies. Deflection is a basic principle of physics: A ball struck with an angled face will start moving in the direction the face is pointing.

As for the swing path, the angle of the face relative to the path the club takes through impact can create sidespin on the ball that makes it veer off its starting line. If the face is open to, or angled to the right of, the swing path, the ball will curve to the right. If the face is closed to, or angled to the left of, the path, the ball will curve to the left. This is where the best players, through the variables listed earlier—grip, stance, alignment, face angle—have built patterns to propel the ball in a predictable direction whether or not the face is square to the target or even close to square.

Think of the swing path as a line moving in one of the three general directions: (1) across the ball from out to in, (2) across the ball from in to out, or (3) straight. To illustrate these directions, think of the tennis stroke: Out to in would be a stroke from high-right to low-left through impact; in to out would be low-left to high-right; and straight would be on a line directly toward the target. A number of factors can influence the path of the club, which we'll discuss in later chapters. For now understand that the angle of the clubface must correspond to the path in a calculable way so the golfer can control the initial start line of the ball and its curve.

Once again, the three fundamentals are: (1) hitting the ground in the same place every time, (2) having enough power to play the course, and (3) being able to match the clubface to the swing path to control shot direction. Working on these fundamentals—in order—is the fastest way to develop your shot-making skills.

STACK & TILT: THE BASIC FORM

AARON BADDELEY

I'm very analytical, so before I ever practiced with Mike and Andy we sat down and talked about the golf swing for hours. They told me how you have to stay centered and how the hands have to move in on the backswing, and here's why. It made sense to me. I thought, Why wouldn't I swing this way?

I used to set my head behind the ball at address, and then shift a little more to the right on the backswing. They got me to stay over the ball going back, to keep my hands in, and to move my tailbone forward coming down. The changes for me were fairly simple, so once I understood them, I was able to put them into play pretty quickly. I think all good ball-strikers naturally do three or four of the things they teach. It's physics, and you can't cheat physics.

People always tell me my swing looks very simple, which is great to hear. Under pressure, simple is better. The biggest change I've seen is better distance control because of the consistency of the strike. My bad shots are not nearly as bad as they used to be. Winning at Hilton Head in 2006, on a tight course with small greens, was proof that my control was better than ever. I never could have contended there the year before.

Can you do Stack & Tilt? Yes. If you're playing golf now, you can do the things that constitute our model. At the root of Stack & Tilt are a few distinguishing moves: Tilt your spine to the left on the backswing and to the right on the downswing, swing your arms inward and around your body, and thrust your lower body upward through impact. You might never have thought of these moves, but in large part they separate most good players from poor players. And they don't require any special physical skills. Try them without a club:

►Standing upright with your hands at your sides, tilt your upper body to the left so that your head moves outside your left leg. Make sure your hips stay in place, without your right hip shifting to the right. That's your spine tilt to the left on the backswing. Now move your spine back to vertical and slide your hips to the left without moving your head—that's the downswing spine tilt. These moves help keep you centered over the ball, which promotes consistent contact, our first fundamental.

↑ Two views of how the spine angle should change during the backswing. From setup (1), the golfer should straighten the spine (2), tilt to the left (3), and turn (4).

Stack & Tilt: The Basic Form

►From your setup position without a club, stand up to vertical. This is how your spine should extend or stretch on the backswing to keep you from dipping as you tilt to the left. Now flex back down to the setup; that's the downswing posture as you approach impact. Stand up straight again, this time stretching your spine a little past vertical; that's the follow-through. This extension allows your body to keep turning through the shot.

↑ The coordination of these movements—straightening the spine from the forward tilt at address (1), tilting to the left (2), and turning (3)—allows the shoulders to turn in a circle, promoting solid contact.

The Stack and Tilt Swing

►Standing upright, turn your shoulders to the right about 45 degrees. That's the shoulder turn. Many golfers are led to believe that the shoulders must turn 90 degrees, but as you'll see, we increase the hip turn so the shoulders have to rotate only 45 degrees independently to reach the full 90. Golfers who don't understand this think they're not flexible enough to make a proper shoulder turn, which sends them off to the gym on a quest to gain a greater range of motion.

↑ If you can turn your shoulders at least 45 degrees without turning your hips, you can make a full 90-degree shoulder turn when you add the proper hip turn.

►Standing upright, bend your knees downward and straighten them. This flexing and extension raises the level of the belt and allows your hips to continue turning forward through the shot. It's particularly important for the lead knee to be able to flex and straighten with weight on it. You must understand that the body has a limited capacity to turn while in flexion, both on the backswing and the downswing. Many golfers mistake this difficulty for a lack of flexibility.

→ **The simple act of straightening your legs on the downswing will release your hips from their downward tilt and allow them to keep turning through the shot.**

The Stack and Tilt Swing

►Standing upright, move your left arm across your chest 45 degrees, keeping it straight. This supplies an upward element to the backswing. Now bend your right elbow 90 degrees—another upward element in the backswing—and join your hands. These moves serve to elevate the club going back without the arms lifting off the chest.

← As the spine tilts to the left during the backswing, the left arm moves 45 degrees across the chest, supplying the upward motion going back.

These motions are simple to perform, made simpler here because your body isn't in the tilted angle required to play golf. Coordinating these moves begins with understanding how they work, without a club in your hands. There is nothing strenuous about reaching these positions; they become complicated when extraneous moves are added, which is the case with many swing models.

Another question we get a lot is, Am I flexible enough to use Stack & Tilt? The answer again is yes. The conventional swing actually requires more flexibility than Stack & Tilt does. Look at the hip and shoulder turns, one major flexibility issue. Many golfers are told to resist with their hips as they turn their shoulders on the backswing, as if they were coiling the body like a spring. The problem with that is that few people are flexible enough to hold their hips in place and make a significant shoulder turn. Our model frees up the hips to maximize rotation, because that allows the shoulders to turn fully. As we just said, when the hips turn 45 degrees, the shoulders have to turn only another 45 to get to 90.

Poor understanding sometimes leads golfers to believe they have a flexibility problem. When asked if they're flexible enough, probably 90 percent of golfers would say they are not, and this is used as a crutch. They hit bad shots, lack distance, whatever, and they say they don't have the body for the game. They get discouraged, all because of bad information. Look at great players like Nicklaus, Stadler, Colin Montgomerie, Tom Lehman—all have had great careers but don't measure up to the flexibility standards that some people consider essential.

Stack & Tilt also relies less on timing. Golfers have long been taught that the body turns back level and the arms swing upright. The problem there is that if the arms lift off the rib cage going back, they have to get back on the body for the downswing so everything can move together through impact. This blending of the horizontal turn and the vertical arm swing is a difficult maneuver for most golfers. Stack & Tilt keeps the arms on the chest throughout the backswing and downswing, creating a flatter arm swing and, more important, a much more repeatable motion.

HOW TO TRY STACK & TILT

We're going to approach the instruction in this section just as we do with a new student, by dispensing the basic pieces of the swing one by one in a certain order. This is important for two reasons: (1) It will help keep you from trying to assimilate too many things at once; (2) it will help you to see how each piece individually affects the flight of the ball.

Just as we discussed the fundamentals in the previous chapter in priority order—contact, power, direction—we've ordered these swing pieces to match them. In other words, the first pieces we describe below contribute the most to contact, the pieces after that mainly concern power, and the final pieces involve direction issues. Of course, some of the pieces affect all three of the fundamentals, so the order reflects how much they influence each one. Once you learn to start hitting the ball solidly, you can add pieces that increase power. When power is sufficient, you can start working on pieces that determine direction.

Following this procedure, you will see how each additional piece contributes to the shots you're hitting. There is no set amount of time for working on each piece (although we will suggest a practice regimen at the end of the chapter), but be careful not to jump ahead in the sequence. If at any point you start to slip in an area already covered, backtrack and focus your attention on the appropriate piece. This progression will ensure that you develop your technique in the most efficient manner.

In a short period of time, you'll see you can hit the ball consistently well without changing many of the so-called conventional fundamentals—grip, posture, alignment, and so on. That's not to say those elements will not require adjustment later, but only that they are not the first things you need to address to hit dramatically better shots. We're not simplifying the golf swing into a short list of swing mechanics; what we are doing is putting some organization to the swing so you can advance faster.

THE FIRST PIECES

Learning the basic form and then building from it is the most effective approach to improvement. As you progress, the basic form is still there, and detail is added to tighten the shot pattern. This is the fastest and most lasting way to develop skill, as long as you understand what's happening at each stage before adding sophistication.

The following are the first pieces, in order, that you should focus on when trying Stack & Tilt for the first time. If we had only a few words to describe the swing, these are what they would be. In fact, based on our experience, these areas are the biggest differentiators between good players and bad. Here they are:

1. Weight forward

2. Left shoulder down

3. Hands in

4. Back leg straight

5. Arms straight

6. Butt under torso

Weight forward

Setting more weight on the front foot at address helps you accomplish two things: You'll hit the ground after the ball, and you won't cut across the ball from out to in through impact. Not only should you favor the front foot at the start, but you should keep the weight forward throughout the swing. The more forward the weight is at impact, the farther forward the low point of the swing will tend to be. This is the most important factor for ensuring consistently solid contact with the ball.

← The weight should be at least 55/45 on the front foot at address.

The second benefit of keeping the weight forward is that you'll be more likely to hit the ball from in to out. The more the weight stays forward, the longer the club swings outward and the better the chance you'll start the ball to the right and hit a draw.

Left shoulder down

Turning the left shoulder downward at the start instead of more level helps to keep the center of the shoulders in place, which is one of the key moves in Stack & Tilt. With the shoulder center fixed, the precision with which the club hits the ground increases. Aside from promoting consistent contact, a stable axis for the shoulder turn also helps keep the path of the hands and arms tracing the correct circular arc. Picture a compass used for drawing circles, with the center of the shoulders being the needle and hands being the pencil that orbits around the fixed center. It should be clear that turning the shoulders without any side-to-side movement off the ball has multiple benefits. Imagine a spike running through the top of your spine and then planted in the ground in front of you, so that all you can do is turn around that stable axis. A fixed shoulder center means the swing will tend to bottom out wherever the weight is at address. If the weight is forward, as prescribed above, the club will generally hit the ground after hitting the ball.

The side tilt to the left (below, left) allows the shoulder center to stay in place as the body turns (below, right). Tilting left also keeps the player in the same inclination toward the ball (left).

The Stack and Tilt Swing

A fixed shoulder center allows the shoulders to turn in a circle, which also contributes to power, because the shoulders have a greater rotation capacity when they simply turn, instead of shifting and turning. The greater the shoulder rotation on the backswing, the more the shoulders can accelerate on the downswing, generating more speed and power.

Hands in

Swinging the hands inward on the backswing is another source of power, because of a physics principle called *angular momentum*. Remember the field-goal kicker: He knows that he can swing his leg faster on an arc than in a straight line. When the hands go back to the inside, they are inclined to take an inside path returning to the ball, thereby accessing the speed benefit of angular momentum. Conversely, a swing in which the hands go straight back and the clubhead traces a straight line off the ball would greatly inhibit the golfer's ability to generate power.

↓ **The hands and club must move inward to access the power of swinging on a circular arc.**

Keeping the hands in also prevents you from cutting across the ball from out to in, because the club is swinging outward on the downswing. This promotes a shot that starts to the right and increases your chances of hitting a draw, the preferred ball flight. Look at it this way: Golf is played with the body in a tilted angle, and the hands and club will naturally swing on an arc that moves inward around the body, unless they are forced to move in a straight line.

Back leg straight

Straightening the back leg during the backswing allows the hips to turn more, which allows the shoulders to also turn more. Just as the left shoulder should turn downward, so should the left hip. This leads to greater hip rotation going back, which creates the potential for more acceleration and power coming down. This is a function of the back leg straightening. Remember, the goal is to maximize the body rotation on the backswing to set the stage for a faster rotation on the downswing.

↓ **The right knee straightening on the backswing gives the hips freedom to turn.**

NO!

Another benefit of the back leg straightening is that it helps you maintain your inclination toward the ball established at address. To understand this, consider what happens when a player turns his hips and shoulders on a more level plane: His body tends to pull off the ball, away from the target. Staying in the same inclination greatly simplifies the task of returning the club to the ball on a consistent basis.

Arms straight

Keeping the arms straight preserves the radius of the swing arc—a line from the left shoulder to the clubhead—allowing you to hit the ground. Of course, the right arm bends on the backswing and the left arm bends at the finish, but as much as possible, the arms should be kept straight. That distance from the left shoulder to the clubhead must not reach full extension before the ball. If it does, the clubhead will hit behind where it was soled. If the arms bend through impact, the radius shortens, requiring a compensation, such as dipping or dropping the right shoulder, for you to catch the ball solidly. Masses of golfers bend both arms too soon through the ball because they sense that the low point of the swing is too far back, so they bend the arms to try to avoid hitting the ground behind the ball.

↓ **Stretching the spine through the shot allows the arms to stay straight. Failure to stretch causes the hips to stop turning; then the arms must bend to avoid hitting behind the ball.**

Straight arms also help prevent you from hitting across the ball from out to in; the club cannot approach the ball from the inside if your elbows are bending on the downswing. In fact, if the swing radius gets short through impact because your arms are bending, the club can only swing from out to in. Full extension of the arms is one of the primary factors allowing the club to continue to swing out to the ball for a draw.

Butt under torso

On the backswing the goal is to essentially turn the hips in a circle, but on the downswing you must push the hips forward and upward to keep them turning. The feeling is that the butt "tucks" under the torso as the hips slide toward the target. This is a major power move because pushing the hips forward and upward releases them from their tilt toward the ball, which increases their rotation capacity and, therefore, allows them to continue to turn through the shot. Remember, your ability to turn is limited when your body is in flexion. The best golfers have learned to keep the hips turning through and to use the ground as a springboard like a jumper by tucking the butt under the torso.

→ **Champion golfers use the ground for power by straightening their legs and tucking the butt under the torso, which allows the spine to extend.**

LEARN THE BASIC FORM
IN THIRTY MINUTES

Because Stack & Tilt contradicts much of what is taught about the golf swing, it is important that you approach these first swings with an open mind and a willingness to focus on one piece at a time. As you progress through the moves described above, you should see improvement as prescribed by the fundamentals: solid contact first, then more distance, then better control of direction.

Here is the basic progression in a thirty-minute practice session:

1. With a middle iron, hit ten balls, focusing on keeping the weight on the front foot;

2. Hit the next ten balls with the weight forward and the left shoulder turning down on the backswing;

3. Hit the next ten balls with the weight forward, left shoulder down, and the hands swinging in;

4. Hit the next ten with the weight forward, shoulder down, hands in, and the butt tucking under the torso through impact;

5. Hit the next ten with the weight forward, shoulder down, hands in, butt tucked, and arms staying straight to the finish.

Using this progression, you should begin to see dramatic improvement in the consistency and quality of contact. You're learning to compress the ball at impact with a downward strike and to keep your shoulder center in place, which fixes the low point of the swing for predictable contact. Power and direction, although more sophisticated elements, should also start to improve.

After a while, you'll naturally want to know how far forward your weight should be, how much your left shoulder should turn down, and how far your hands should move in. These details will be addressed in the next two chapters. The goal here is to provide a quick study of the pieces that constitute the basic form. Refinement of these pieces will determine how well you develop the swing. Remember, these moves and positions set up everything that follows. This is not an exercise but a starting point.

Troubleshooting

Although these basic moves are not physically demanding, some players struggle to achieve them adequately at the start. This is usually due to a lack of sufficient attention to a particular piece or a strong predisposition in a certain area, such as thinking the weight has to shift to the right on the backswing. These factors can have a negative impact on your capacity to quickly incorporate the pieces.

With practice and diligence, anyone can easily learn the basic form. But as with any swing technique, players who have a clear understanding of what they're trying to do, and how to recognize it by watching the ball, improve faster. There are four areas in which we see the greatest separation between players at higher and lower skill levels. Here are the typical problems that less-skilled players demonstrate:

1. The left shoulder does not turn down enough on the backswing, causing the shoulder turn to be too level.

Here's a spectrum illustrating how the spine tilting to the left controls the downward path of the left shoulder. We prescribe image C, above, for iron shots.

The Stack and Tilt Swing

2. The hands do not swing inward enough and/or for long enough on the backswing.

3. The hips move to the right on the backswing or don't slide forward fast enough on the downswing.

4. The arms bend too soon in the follow-through.

These faulty positions can be tough to identify without an instructor's help, so let's look at the most common mis-hits and errant ball flights we see with players trying Stack & Tilt for the first time. Applying the corresponding adjustment to the problems described can keep you on track and the basic form intact.

Problem: Hitting the ground behind the ball

Adjustment: You probably haven't moved enough weight to the front foot at address. Beginning and developing players can put 60 to 70 percent of their weight forward and keep it there throughout the swing (right). This will move the low point of your swing forward to produce a descending strike and flush contact.

Problem: Not hitting the ground at all

Adjustment: One common problem we see is golfers making very little wrist hinge on the backswing, which is often caused by the elbows pulling apart. Then the left wrist flexes upward through impact. The opposite should happen: The wrists hinge on the backswing and then return to their address angles through impact, with the arms staying straight into the follow-through. The weight of the club on the downswing unhinges the wrists; no conscious unhinging is necessary.

If the wrists flip the club upward through impact, the elbows tend to pull apart, with the left elbow moving up the rib cage. This usually means the right hand is scooping as a way of helping the ball into the air. You should focus on keeping the space between your elbows constant from address through impact (left). This should keep the club moving downward, with the wrists staying firm. As long as the weight is forward, the club will hit the ball, then the ground.

Problem: Deep divots after impact

Adjustment: Assuming contact is good, this is an easy fix. The hands and arms are probably working correctly; you simply need to tuck the butt quicker through the strike to take some of the steepness out of the swing. The level of your belt should rise by a good few inches through impact. Releasing your hips from their downward tilt toward the ball helps shallow the swing to prevent those steep crashes. Focus on pushing off the ground and straightening your legs as your arms stay straight through the shot (right).

FAQ: How can you create power without shifting your weight?

Stack & Tilt does feature a weight shift: toward the target on the downswing. The idea that you have to shift to the right going back to set up a powerful move into impact is simply false. In fact, that big shift off the ball usually drains power from the swing because it makes it harder to hit the ball solidly. One of the main power sources in the swing is body rotation, maximized by the spine tilt changing at various points of the swing, and it's easier to make a full turn with Stack & Tilt than it is with the traditional shift-and-turn backswing.

Problem: Slicing

Adjustments: Three possible causes here: (1) your hands and arms are not going inward enough on the backswing, leading to an out-to-in path through the ball; (2) your hips are not sliding toward the target enough on the downswing; or (3) the shaft is not leaning forward enough (face-on view) or angled upward enough (downtarget view) through impact.

To fix the first problem, exaggerate the movement of your hands to the inside. Keeping your arm swing shorter on the backswing should also help.

The second problem is usually a result of the upper body rotating too quickly to start the downswing. Focus on moving your hips laterally, pushing more weight onto your front foot (below). When the body starts turning open before the hips move laterally enough, the club is thrown to the outside and the swing path becomes out to in. Thrusting your hips forward and upward will keep the club on an inside path for a draw.

The third problem, the shaft not leaning forward enough (face-on view) or lowering through the ball (downtarget view), often occurs when you roll the club over with your wrists in an attempt to close the clubface. This has the effect of moving the path to the left, more across the ball, which worsens the slice. You need to move the butt end of the grip higher and more forward at address and then focus on maintaining the angle of the right arm to the shaft throughout the downswing.

Problem: Hitting the ball too low

Adjustment: If you're a habitual slicer, you're hitting across the ball with a steep angle of descent probably with a clubface that's closed to the target. (Think back to our discussion on the face angle determining starting direction: Slicers need a closed clubface to start the ball left and make room for the curve.) The butt end of the grip has to be more forward and upward at address, which presets the swing path more in to out on the downswing. Once the swing path is from the inside, not across the ball like it is with slicers, the closed clubface takes too much loft off the shot. So open the face more at ad-

FAQ: Isn't a level shoulder turn one of the hallmarks of a good swing?

Turning the shoulders level means they have to pull off of the downward tilt toward the ball they held at address. This requires a change in posture and also leads to the shoulder center shifting away from the target—two moves that are very difficult to overcome. To maintain your inclination toward the ball, the left shoulder should turn downward to start the swing. This also starts the club tracking on the proper inward path, with the arms staying connected to the rib cage, and not lifting onto a more vertical plane. Remember, turning the shoulders in a circle without the center moving and swinging on an inside path are two traits of the great ball-strikers.

dress, and weaken your left-hand grip by turning it more toward the target. These changes will combat the closed face and put more loft on the shot.

← **Moving the handle farther forward promotes hitting from the inside.**

FAQ: Shouldn't the club swing straight back and straight through?

Trying to swing the club on a straight line makes your arms pull away from your body and move the club too vertically. Traditional instruction says the arms swing up and down, like a Ferris wheel, and the body turns horizontally, like a merry-go-round. The problem with that advice is that those are competing forces that need to come together on the downswing. It's very difficult to reconcile those two moves. As a result, they account for a lot of the inconsistent contact seen among average golfers.

Problem: Hooking

Adjustment: Four things to check here, and the first three are easy—all at address. First, the ball might be too far back in the stance; it should be a couple of inches in front of center for a middle iron. Second, the clubface might be too closed, so be sure to aim the face to the right of the target. Third, the left hand is probably rotated into a strong position; it should be turned only slightly away from the target. The fourth possible cause of the hook is your arms pulling off your torso on the through-swing and swinging too vertically to the finish. This raises the butt end of the shaft and shoots the swing path out to the right (below, right). Focus on keeping the upper part of your arms connected to your body all the way through (below, left). This will keep your hands and the club on the correct circular arc around the body and counteract a hook.

These fixes address only the most common problems we see with golfers starting out with Stack & Tilt. There is a more detailed discussion of faults and fixes in Chapter 8. Our objective in this section has been to provide a quick lesson on the swing's basic form so you can start to understand the overall motion. In the next two chapters we'll refine the instruction and add detail.

FAQ: Isn't the Stack & Tilt Swing too steep for hitting the driver?

Two adjustments in the driver setup will shallow out the swing: widening the stance and playing the ball farther forward. With the feet wider, the hips should be slightly more forward than they are with the irons. (The body weight is 55/45 on the left foot with the irons and 60/40 with the driver.) This setup, plus tucking the butt through impact to straighten the spine, helps shallow the club's approach to the ball. With the ball up in the stance, the clubhead is swinging level to the ground, less descending, at impact. In addition, the longer shaft in the driver naturally makes the club swing flatter, more around the body, which also reduces the steepness of the swing.

THE SETUP AND BACKSWING

MIKE WEIR

In July 2006 I was at an event with Jack Nicklaus and asked him what he remembered most from what his longtime teacher, Jack Grout, taught him. He said it was how Mr. Grout used to stand in front of him when he was a kid and hold his hair while he hit balls. This kept him from moving his head during the swing, and he said when he did this he felt like his left shoulder was turning down to the ball.

About a month after that, I talked to Andy about my golf swing for the first time, and he said I needed to tilt more to my right on the backswing—toward the target, because I'm a lefty. That sounded a lot like what Jack was saying, so I tried it, and I could immediately see how it led to better compression on the ball and a more pene-trating shot. I'd been struggling with back pain and my contact was pretty sloppy, all over the clubface, and keeping my spine centered made a huge difference.

The biggest challenge for me with the swing has been staying centered on the downswing. I have a tendency to lean away from the target a little, which can make me hit up on my longer clubs.

Now I can catch a long iron solid and send it high, instead of hitting low shots that come off the bottom of the clubface. I also went through a period where I was trying to be too perfect with the positions that Andy and Mike were teaching me, but I eventually started adapting them to my swing.

I found it easy to do on the range, but of course the key is taking it to the course. If one round stands out as eye-opening for me it was the final round of the Phoenix event in late 2007. I controlled the ball perfectly that day. The wind was blowing about thirty miles an hour, and I was holding the ball into those crosswinds. I shot 68 on a day when the scoring average was like 73, and won. I was controlling my shots, and I knew exactly how.

I n the last chapter we looked at the broad concepts of Stack & Tilt. Those elements are the foundation of the swing and do not change, regardless of skill level. Here we add the detail, such as when those moves occur and to what degree. Where relevant, we discuss how Stack & Tilt is different from the conventional swing. After reading this section, you'll have a detailed road map for how the club and the different parts of the body move from the setup to the top of the backswing.

Before we get started, we'll say it again: Golf is played on a tilted angle, with the upper body flexed toward the ball, and because of this forward tilt, the club must swing around the body in a circular arc, never straight back or straight through. The golf swing is not like tossing horseshoes or playing croquet, where the motion traces a straight line; the golf swing is a circle that moves the club around the body. The hands swing on an arc, and the clubhead swings on a larger arc; picture these motions as two concentric circles. We will refer to these circles often because they combine to form the basic shape of the golf swing.

← The clubhead and the hands should move in concentric circles around the body.

↓ Players who draw the ball move the weight and handle forward (below, left). Players who fade it move the weight and handle back (below, right).

THE SETUP

Starting at address, we will work our way from the ground up. Keep in mind that strict adherence to any of these variables is not necessary to playing golf well. Use these instructions as guidelines over the long term, but apply only the most significant elements as they pertain to your swing. In other words, don't get fixated on, say, how your right foot is positioned at address if 80 percent of your weight is behind the ball. These factors do not carry equal weight, but it is important to know the ideal positions for each. Learning what all the pieces do will help you determine what is happening in your swing, and what adjustments you need to make. Getting your swing priorities right is how you will progress fastest.

THE FEET AND LEGS

As the body's only contact with the ground, the feet (and legs) serve several critical functions during the swing. Most importantly, they provide stability for the turn and create a platform for generating power. Your feet should be rotated outward 10 to 20 degrees each as a baseline position, which allows the hips to turn more than they would if your feet were straight out.

← Stack & Tilt setup: feet rotated outward, weight 55/45 on front side, hands in line with inside of left leg.

Moving up, your knees should be flexed forward, over your toes. This forward flexing engages the ankles and makes it feel as if your feet are being pushed into the ground. Downward pressure stabilizes the body, creating resistance against the ground. This position is a common differentiator between good and poor players; if you don't have a firm connection with the ground, your hips will tend to slide away from the target on the backswing.

Like the feet, your knees should be rotated outward, but only a few degrees. It is very common to see the right knee rotated inward too much, toward the left. This inward position encourages the spine to tilt away from the target on the downswing, one of the most haphazard moves a golfer can make.

To counter the forward flex in the knees, push your butt back to keep your weight on the centers of your feet from front to back. This tilts the hips, or beltline, at a downward angle to the ground, as viewed from downtarget. From the face-on view, your hip center should be slightly forward of your stance center, about an inch, putting your weight 55/45 on the left side.

→ **Stack & Tilt setup: top part of spine rounded downward, arms hanging nearly vertical, butt of club pointing at top of pants zipper.**

Your torso from the downtarget view should be flexed forward, toward the ball, but your spine should not be in a straight line. Your spine should curve forward slightly, or tilt progressively more from bottom to top, so that your neck is angled more toward the ball than your lower back. This rounding of the spine serves two purposes. First, it allows your shoulders to roll inward and your arms to pinch against your torso. Second, it tilts your head downward so you can see the ball without straining to look out of the bottoms of your eyes.

The Stack and Tilt Swing

From the face-on view, your spine should be nearly vertical, with the notch in the sternum just forward of the center of your stance. This vertical alignment of the shoulders over the hips makes the body appear "stacked" at address. Many teachers advocate tilting the upper body away from the target in the setup, which presets a weight shift to the back foot and a turn that's too level to the ground. This is one of the main differences between conventional teaching and Stack & Tilt.

← **The shoulders are directly over the hips, creating a "stacked" address position.**

What it feels like: setup

AARON BADDELEY

When I was learning the setup, I would get over the ball, and then stand up straight, as if I was just talking to someone. You'd never tilt to the right if you were addressing someone. Then I'd bend forward from the hips and just unlock my knees. That got me over the ball in a stacked position.

We like the shoulder alignment to be square, or parallel to the target line. It is very common for amateur players to have the shoulders, hips, and knees turned open, or aligned too far to the left, especially when the ball is forward in the stance for the longer clubs. When open alignment is combined with the weight being back and the butt end of the club being back—two common setup faults—the golfer is doomed to swing across the ball.

The upper parts of your arms should be tight to your chest, with both arms straight—another trademark position of Stack & Tilt. Your elbows should be rotated inward a few degrees, with your arms forming a triangle with the line of your shoulders. Viewed downtarget, your arms should hang almost vertically, controlled by the forward tilt of your torso, with your hands out slightly for the driver.

Your hands should be opposite the inside of your left thigh, with the grip of the club over the inside part of your left ankle from your perspective. Combined with the correct ball location, this position creates a slight forward lean of the shaft from the face-on view. The greater this angle, the easier it is to hit down and out at the ball. From the downtarget view, with your torso flexed toward the ball and your arms vertical, the butt of the club points to the top of the pants zipper. This is a baseline position that can be adjusted to promote different ball flights, as we'll discuss later.

This completes the body positions at address for the standard Stack & Tilt setup. You should feel poised and prepared for action, not relaxed. To understand this ready position, consider other sports: If the baseball catcher took a relaxed stance, he would not be able to react to wild pitches; if the defender in basketball relaxed his leg muscles, he would give up a lot of easy layups. You should not feel limp or lazy. We use the term "structural rigidity" to remind golfers that the body must support a heavy load and, therefore, must be stable enough to do so while staying in balance.

What it feels like: setup

CHARLIE WI

To set more weight on my front foot at address, the feeling I use is that my right hip is higher than my left. This presets the hips to turn on a steep downward angle instead of turning back level. Once I got the hip turn right, I stopped shifting my body off the ball in the backswing, and I started striking the ball much more consistently.

BALL POSITION

Amateur golfers often overlook ball position, but to the experienced player it is one of the most important variables to monitor. Ball position, alignment, angle of the clubface, and location of the weight are the main factors in swing direction.

Because the club moves on a circular arc, as we described, the ball must be positioned at a particular point on this arc. We prefer the ball to be slightly on the back side of the arc, so that impact occurs while the club is still swinging outward. This promotes the preferred draw and encourages the correct descent to the ball.

The location of the weight forms a rotational axis for the swing (picture that spike running through your body, discussed earlier, that keeps the swing center in place). Because we prescribe the weight to be 55/45 on the left, the ball should be slightly behind the rotational axis to promote a downward strike. Golfers have been conditioned to see ball position only as it relates to the left foot, but we want you to be aware of ball position relative to the weight and the swing arc.

The Setup and Backswing

That said, if the weight is positioned correctly, the ball should be two balls inside the left heel for a standard middle-iron shot.

The shot pattern we use as a baseline is a slight push-draw. With the weight 55/45 and the ball two balls behind the heel, the club will tend to make contact swinging in to out. The player should move the ball forward for longer clubs, particularly the driver, to help shallow the descent of the clubhead into the ball. Understand that you're more inclined to swing from out to in as the ball moves forward. This is why it is more difficult for amateurs to push-draw their longer clubs: The forward ball position encourages them to cut across the ball, striking it on the front side of the swing arc.

Keep in mind that as the ball moves forward, so must the axis of the turn, so that the club is still moving outward when it strikes the ball. To do this, your hips must slide forward more on the down-swing. This, in turn, increases the spine's side tilt to the right (face-on view) and enables the golfer to keep swinging out at the ball to produce a draw. The weight distribution of the lower body should be slightly more forward with the longer clubs, about 60/40. You need to recognize that there is more hip slide with a driver than with a middle iron, and this shallows the angle of descent and keeps the club moving outward, even to the more forward ball position.

The increased lateral movement of your hips increases your side tilt to your right while keeping the center of your shoulders in place. Most amateurs do not slide the hips far enough and, therefore, hit across the ball with steeper descents on the longer clubs. In short, the amount of hip slide must match the club: more for long clubs, less for short clubs.

What it feels like: setup

MIKE WEIR

I used to tilt my head behind the ball and play from an open stance. When I squared up my body and got centered, I felt like my head was a foot in front of the ball. It was definitely a weird feeling at first, but my contact improved right away. I started hitting everything in the middle of the face, so I immediately believed in the concept of starting and staying over the ball.

THE CLUBFACE AND GRIP

The clubface should point at the intended starting line of the shot. For our baseline stroke pattern (push-draw), the face at address should be a few degrees open to the target. Because a push-draw has a slight right-to-left curve that does not cross the target, this open clubface starts the ball to the right to allow for the curve.

The grip has a few key variables, but you have some latitude. Don't change your grip in the beginning without consideration of the desired swing path or clubface alignment at impact. But there are a few baseline grip elements that must be understood. First, the heel pad of your left hand should sit on top of the grip. This creates downward pressure on top of the club and encourages the left wrist to hinge properly during the swing. Second, your left thumb should extend one joint past your left forefinger. Many poor players set the left forefinger too far down the grip, thereby restricting the wrist hinge. The correct "hitchhiker" thumb position promotes the full, powerful hinging of the wrist on the backswing. Third, the hollow or dimple that forms on top of your wrist when you raise your left thumb provides another important checkpoint. You should position it nearly in line with the top of the grip, slightly to the right of center from your perspective. This will rotate your left hand slightly away from the target.

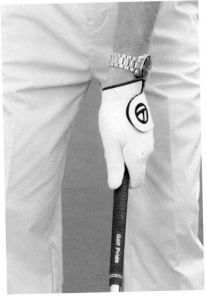

The club is held in the fingers of the left hand, with the heel pad on top of the grip.

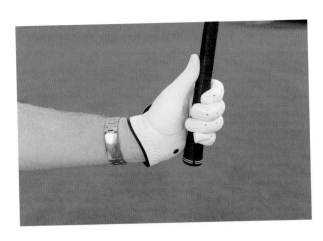

A few references also exist for your right hand. The grip should sit along the base of the fingers, so that the first joint of your forefinger pushes against the back of the club. As your right hand completes the grip, it covers your left thumb, which is turned slightly to the right. This connection between your hands forms a pressure point that should not change during the swing. Finally, your right pinky finger should hook around back, between the first two fingers of your left hand, forming the classic Vardon, or overlapping, grip.

→ **The right hand grips with the fingers and covers the left thumb.**

Again, we emphasize that you should not change your grip just to conform to our baseline standard. The grip and clubface alignment have to be compatible with your swing and desired ball flight. Use the elements of grip and clubface alignment described above as a guide, but do not change just for the sake of change. We'll discuss the role of the grip and the face angle in producing various ball flights in Chapter 6.

THE BACKSWING

One common question we hear is, What starts the backswing? The best way to approach that topic is to think of the golf swing as an ocean liner, not a canoe: It has many parts moving at a time that make up the whole instead of one small part. You need a comprehensive overview of the motion to understand how to direct the various parts of the body to create the correct sequence of the swing. So consider it the brain that starts the swing: Clear intentions simplify execution.

THE SHOULDERS

One of the main functions of the backswing is to turn the shoulders in a circle on a downward angle with the shoulder center staying in place. This provides precision to the path of the hands and the club. It also creates balance to support your rotation and gives the backswing its around-the-body shape, which is a major source of power. Many golfers have played well while moving the center of the shoulder turn back, but these are highly adapted players who have learned to compensate for this move. Shifting the shoulder center off the ball not only creates less power, it also results in erratic geometry.

The way we see it, you have a choice: Turn your shoulders in a circle around a stable center, or sway going back and then lunge forward. The latter requires you to master the art of getting the forward lunge to equal the backward sway. This is extremely complicated and highly unpredictable. Therefore, we teach turning the shoulders in a circle while keeping the center in place.

For the center of the shoulder turn to stay stable, the left shoulder itself must trace a circular path. Turning the shoulder downward enough on the backswing is one of the main differences between good and poor players. Many golfers at some point in their backswings lose the downward component of the shoulder turn, which causes the head and the shoulder center to drift back. To rotate correctly, the left shoulder must turn downward and inward at a consistent rate.

For the left shoulder to turn in a circle and at a right angle to the spine, the spine must change its flex: It cannot stay in its original forward tilt toward the ball. To release this flex without moving the center of the shoulder turn is the challenge of the pivot. The spine first tilts to the left, which gives the left shoulder the freedom to go downward, and must continue to tilt left throughout the backswing. If at any point the spine stops tilting to the left, the left shoulder will level out, moving the center of the shoulders back. When you get to the top of the backswing, you should be in a full side tilt when viewed down-target, meaning you have tilted to the left as far as you can.

For the shoulders to turn in a circle, the left shoulder also must turn in a circle (above), not shift behind the ball (right).

The Stack and Tilt Swing

This is difficult for some golfers to recognize because they are usually seeing the swing from a single angle. When viewed face-on, the spine stays vertical during the backswing and, therefore, no tilt to the left is visible. To see the spine tilt, the observer has to move with the swing. Starting from the face-on view, the spine at address is vertical, but at halfway back, the observer would have to move to a three-quarter angle (halfway between face-on and downtarget) to see the spine tilting to the left.

Notice how the spine goes from vertical at setup (1) to tilting left (2) to tilting toward the ball (3) when the perspective moves with the swing.

To recognize the left tilt at the top of the swing, the observer would have to be looking downtarget, where the left tilt is seen as a tilt toward the ball, just as the spine was at address. It might appear that the golfer has simply stayed in his address tilt, but he has actually tilted about 30 degrees to the left to maintain his inclination to the ball. If the golfer stayed in his address tilt as he turned back, the left shoulder would not go down. The center of the shoulder turn would move to the right, over the right foot.

There is another aspect of the spine action that must happen on the backswing: The spine must rise up out of its address tilt toward the ball. To understand this, look at it this way: If you only tilted to the left and turned your shoulders, your head would move down, changing your distance from the ball. So as you tilt to the left, you must also fully stretch your spine, from tilted forward to vertical. Again, this might look from the face-on view like you are simply staying in your address posture, but you are actually straightening your spine to counteract the left tilt. This is what allows you to maintain your relationship to the ball. Yes, this sounds complicated, but we see amateurs incorporating these spine actions very quickly. Why are they necessary? They constitute the only way you can turn back while keeping your shoulder center in place, which is the number-one key to making solid contact with the ball. Once the shoulder center moves, contact becomes unpredictable.

We often compare this straightening of the spine to the Fosbury

Flop, where the high jumper arches his back to clear the bar. You must stretch out your spine as you tilt to the left to keep the shoulder center stable. So tilt to the left and stand up, and you'll stay right on the ball.

↙ **This rear view of Sam Snead shows the centered shoulder turn, the high right hip, and the straightening of the spine.**

Ben Hogan included in his famous book *Five Lessons: The Modern Fundamentals of Golf* an illustration that shows the center of the shoulders closer to the target than the center of the hips at the top of the backswing. He also drew diagrams of this concept in his writings and reportedly said that the farthest point from the target at the top of the backswing is the belt buckle. This comes from the full straightening of the spine all the way to the bottom vertebrae.

What it feels like: steady head

TOMMY ARMOUR III

I have a tendency to sway off the ball a little, so the feeling I use to stay in place is that my head goes to my left and down a little on the backswing. When I feel this, my head is really just staying in place.

David Leadbetter's book on Hogan's swing, *The Fundamentals of Hogan,* highlighted this concept under the term "reverse pivot." But old photos of Snead, Nicklaus, and Palmer also demonstrate the move. These pictures and many others give historical precedent to the spine action we teach. The problem is, most instructors never tell anyone to tilt the spine to the left under the pretense that it is a reverse pivot. So golfers are allowed to retain their forward tilt and, therefore, move the center of the shoulders to the right. Plenty of top golfers today tilt their spines to the left: Sergio Garcia, Colin Montgomerie, and Fred Couples actually tilt more left than we prescribe, and they are three of the best drivers in golf—a fact that is lost on those who label this a reverse pivot or say it does not work with the driver.

Straightening the spine and tilting it to the left also has an effect on other actions. First, it moves your hands and arms upward and inward, controlling the initial path of the swing. Consider this: Your hands and arms must move in three dimensions—backward, inward, and upward. The backward and inward come primarily from the turning torso, and the spine tilt to the left supplies a major portion of the upward movement.

⬆ **When the left shoulder turns down and the spine tilts left, the hands and club ascend properly.**

The Stack and Tilt Swing

Furthermore, straightening the spine frees your shoulders and hips to turn more on the backswing. If you stay in your forward tilt as you swing back, you severely restrict your ability to turn your shoulders. This has a major effect on golfers who are told by instructors that they don't have enough flexibility to turn their shoulders. They are sometimes put on elaborate workout programs to increase their flexibility, which makes the game seem too difficult to play.

To understand the left-tilting and raising of the spine in a simple phrase, consider how we tell juniors to turn the left shoulder: Down and in, under the chin. Remember, one of the primary objectives of the backswing is to turn the shoulders in a circle, and you do this by fully straightening the spine and tilting left. This is one of the distinguishing traits of the Stack & Tilt player, and it allows the hands and club to move on the correct arcs and preserve the proper geometry of the swing.

What it feels like: spine tilt

CHARLIE WI

A great image for me on the backswing is thinking of my body as the Leaning Tower of Pisa. When the right hip gets higher going back and the right leg straightens, the feeling is that the spine tilts toward the target. In reality the spine stays vertical (from the face-on view), but if you're used to tilting away from the target, as I was, this image should help you.

THE ARMS

As your spine tilts to the left on the backswing, it produces the initial upward and inward movement of the arms. The left arm begins to cross the chest, creating another lever in the swing. Picture this left-arm action from directly overhead: At address the left arm extends at about a 90-degree angle off the chest, and as the left arm swings back that angle closes significantly, to approximately 45 degrees. Your hands, which were approximately twenty inches from your right shoulder in the setup, are now ten inches from the shoulder. This is a result of the left arm moving across the chest and the right arm flexing 90 degrees. It's commonly taught that the hands need to stay extended on the backswing, away from the head. We agree, in that the right elbow should not fold past 90 degrees, but the hands should not finish the backswing opposite the right ear or higher than the head. They should be four to six inches behind the right shoulder from the downtarget view, with the left arm parallel to the line of the shoulders when the club reaches the top. That confirms the correct inside path.

Note that this inward and upward backswing motion has occurred without any lifting of the arms off the torso. When the arms and spine tilt work correctly going back, the right elbow is very close to the right side—it starts three inches from the rib cage and maintains that distance all the way to the top. This proves that the hand path has moved well to the inside of the target line and the arms have not

→ **Top of the backswing: The left arm matches the shoulder line and the right elbow is still close to the rib cage—no lifting of the arms.**

The Stack and Tilt Swing

lifted to complete the backswing. The left arm should ride on the torso, hugging the chest closely, a position that will become a major power factor in the downswing.

What it feels like: takeaway

MIKE WEIR

People always ask me about my waggle. I used to waggle the club straight back, with my right arm, my leading arm, parallel to the target line, but I've changed that. Now my right arm goes well inside the line, 20 or 30 degrees. It's the feel I want to start my swing. But if I keep my spine more vertical (face-on view) as I swing back, my hands track to the inside. I don't really have to focus on them.

THE WRISTS

As the arms swing back, the wrists should hinge continuously to the top, creating a 90-degree angle with the left arm. Your wrists should not stay rigid during the takeaway or, at the other extreme, hinge fully during the first part of the backswing. If the wrists hinge too early or too late, the clubface will tend to rotate erratically and, therefore, stray from square during the backswing. This would require a correction or compensation somewhere in the downswing for the clubface to be square at impact. So hinge your wrists gradually on the backswing, eventually forming a right angle between your left arm and the shaft.

There is another pair of wrist angles, however, that contributes to an accurate delivery of the club: the side bending, or back-and-forth action, of the wrists. To see the difference between wrist hinge and side bend, grip a club and hold it up in front of you. Bob the clubhead straight up and down—that's the wrist hinge. Then try moving it from side to side, like a dog wags its tail—that's the side bend. This side-to-side movement is rarely discussed, but it can have a profound impact on the path and the low point of the swing, potentially affecting contact and direction.

Our advice on the side bending of the wrists is simple: Don't do it. Whatever side angles you see at address—with most players a practically straight line from the left arm down the shaft and an angle between the right arm and the shaft—should not change during the swing. (Many Stack & Tilt swingers refer to the side bend in the right wrist as the flying wedge, a term used in *The Golfing Machine*.) The only acceptable wrist action is the vertical hinging and unhinging. This is purely an up-and-down action, though it might appear to be side to side because the swing is on a tilted plane. You should set the side angles at address and maintain them as the wrists hinge and unhinge.

→ **The hips should turn more to increase backswing rotation and prevent the arms from lifting.**

THE HAND PATH

We have discussed how your hands should move inward on the backswing, but let's add a little detail as to how much. The hands should begin their journey a few inches in front of your left leg. As they start back, powered by the turn of the torso, they pass through the body at the belt, from the downtarget view. From there, the hands continue moving on an inward angle so that they're about six inches behind your right shoulder when they reach the top.

← Varying degrees of inward hand path: We prescribe the hands passing through the belt from this angle.

What it feels like: hand path

AARON BADDELEY

To get my hands swinging more to the inside on the backswing, I used to think about setting my hands at the top behind my right shoulder instead of above it. For me, that thought took care of the backswing; it got my hands moving on the correct inside path.

THE HIPS AND KNEES

We've said that straightening your right knee allows the hips and the shoulders to continue turning on the backswing, but this important action merits further discussion. The flexing of your left knee and straightening of your right allows your hips to turn on a tilted angle so that your right hip is several inches higher than your left when the backswing is complete. If your right knee stayed too flexed, the angle of the hips would ultimately flatten. Then the hips would stop turning, the shoulders would stop turning, and the shoulder center would shift away from the target.

Consider a couple of checkpoints for the rate at which this flexing and straightening of the legs occurs. At setup both knees should be flexed forward a few inches, but as the club starts back, the right knee immediately begins to straighten and the left knee to flex more. When the club reaches the top the left knee should be flexed several inches toward the ball and the right knee essentially straight. Exact measurements depend on the length of your legs and the club you're using, but what is universally true is the relationship of flexing and straightening and how they increase your hip turn.

➜ **Going back, the left knee flexes several inches toward the ball as the right knee straightens.**

The Stack and Tilt Swing

This leg action is one of the moves that give Stack & Tilt its distinct look. With the right leg straight or almost straight and the left knee flexed forward, the hips are free to make a full rotation, which allows the shoulders to turn more. So the leg action increases the overall range of motion on the backswing. This bigger turn is achievable without the shoulder center moving off the ball. The weight still favors the front foot at the top, and can even shift slightly more forward during the backswing. No weight ever shifts to the back foot, eliminating the need to recover at the start of the downswing.

Remember, the most important task on the backswing is to keep the shoulder center in place, because that allows you to control where the club hits the ground. Whatever power you might gain from shifting off the ball comes at the expense of solid contact. Turning the shoulders in a circle is the master key of the Stack & Tilt backswing, and any move that compromises it will inhibit your ability to get back to the ball with precision. Our model creates the simplest possible backswing that also generates sufficient power. Adding a weight shift off the ball can be a power move, but solid contact has to be the first priority.

What it feels like: hip turn

MIKE WEIR

Like a lot of players, I used to keep my back leg flexed on the backswing, which really restricted my hip turn. As a result, my swing would get very upright. When I started letting my back knee straighten, that freed up my hips to turn. I never realized how wound up I could get. That allowed me to use the muscles in my core to generate power, which I understood from my hockey days. I added a lot of speed and distance on all my shots.

THE CLUBFACE

As we said earlier, at address the clubface should be a few degrees open to the target for our baseline push-draw. On the backswing, as the hands and club move inward, the clubface stays square, or 90 degrees, to the path of the swing. This means minimal rotation of the arms and club. Remember, the turning torso controls the circular path the clubface travels on. Keep these two popular checkpoints for clubface position in mind: (1) When the shaft is parallel to the ground on the backswing, the clubface is slightly less than vertical; and (2) when the club reaches the top of the backswing, the clubface matches the angle of the left arm.

→ **At the top, the clubface should match the angle of the left arm.**

THE BACKSWING IN SEQUENCE

Now that we have covered the major pieces of the backswing, let's see how they blend together. At the setup your weight is 55/45 on the left side, and your shoulders are stacked over your hips. Your left shoulder begins turning downward and inward and your spine tilts to the left—this keeps the center of the shoulder turn stable—with no lifting of the arms. At the same time, your spine is straightening to vertical, as seen from the face-on view; if your spine only tilted to the left and didn't straighten, your upper body would dip toward the ball. These spine actions must occur simultaneously, working together to engage the powerful muscles in the back. Your hands are trac-

The Stack and Tilt Swing

ing their circular arc, as your left arm begins to cross your chest and your right arm begins to fold. Your wrists start to hinge from the start, and the angle of the clubface remains square to the arc, almost "toe up" when the shaft reaches parallel to the ground.

As the club continues back, your left shoulder continues its downward turn, keeping the shoulder center stable. Your hips continue to turn, and your left knee and right knee flex and straighten, respectively, to promote hip turn. As your left arm reaches parallel to the ground, it is crossing your chest and the shaft is hinged 90 degrees to the arm. From the downtarget view, your hands pass through the base to the middle of the right biceps, and your weight is still 55/45 because your hips and shoulders are turning in a circle, not shifting off the ball.

⬇ **Stack & Tilt backswing: The right elbow should flex to 90 degrees (below, left) and the left arm should cross the chest without lifting (below, right).**

Near the top of the backswing, your head actually rotates a few degrees to the right but the center of the shoulder turn stays in place. Your eyes are able to stay on the ball simply by moving in their sockets. Your spine has fully stretched or bowed away from the target and has tilted 35 degrees to the left. The continuous left-tilting of the spine has become the forward tilt toward the ball (downtarget view). Your right knee is nearly straight, and your left knee has flexed toward the ball several inches. This has allowed your hips the freedom to turn 45 degrees, with your right hip higher than your left.

Your right arm has flexed 90 degrees and your left arm has crossed your chest 45 degrees. Your hands are about six inches behind your right shoulder from the downtarget view, and your right elbow is three inches from your rib cage, proving that no lifting has occurred. The angle of the clubface matches the angle of your left arm, indicating a square face. Most important, the shoulder center has stayed perfectly still.

← **As the body turns, the continuous left-tilting of the spine becomes the forward tilt toward the ball.**

With the backswing complete, you should feel a rotational tension in your spine. Picture the twisted double helix of the DNA model from high school biology class. Downward pressure on your left knee indicates that your weight has begun to shift to the left while your left knee stays flexed. This is a fully coiled, dynamic position loaded with energy and ready to reverse direction and unwind into impact.

THE DOWNSWING AND FOLLOW-THROUGH

ERIC AXLEY

My first session with the guys was at New Orleans in 2006, my rookie year. Mike came with me to an off-site pro-am on Wednesday, and we squeezed in fifteen minutes on the range before I teed off. Two amazing things happened. First, I could feel immediately that I was compressing the ball better. Second, for maybe the first time in my life I was hitting draws without trying to manufacture them. After two rounds in the event, I was tied for third. I couldn't believe how fast my swing had changed.

One big thing I'd been doing wrong was lifting my arms up in the backswing. It caused me to swing across every ball and hit a lot of pull-cuts. I just couldn't hit a draw. Once we got my weight forward and I learned to keep my arms in, the shape of my swing changed completely: The club stayed low and around my body, and I could hit the ball from the inside. For me, the feeling was that I was swinging my hands back over my back foot and keeping 90 percent of my weight on my front side.

The ultimate validation of what we were working on came at the Texas Open that year. From the 13th hole in the first round to the

2nd hole in the last round, I never had to chip the ball. I hit forty-three greens in a row, every green on Friday and Saturday, and I won my first tour event. If I didn't know it already, I knew it then: Stack & Tilt was the answer for me.

Before we break down the motions of the downswing, let's look at what you have to accomplish as you swing into the ball. Remember, the number-one priority is to make solid contact, and a big part of that comes from keeping the shoulder center in place, just like on the backswing. To maximize power, the body must keep turning through impact. And to control the direction and curve, the hands must swing on a consistent arc and the clubhead must descend into impact unless the ball is teed.

Every player wants to know what starts the downswing. As we'll explain, every part of the body has a role, and which one you should focus on depends on your tendencies. We'll give you the basic structure below, but you might need to correct a faulty downswing, so refer to our discussion on common faults in Chapter 8.

The downswing moves in three directions: forward, outward, and downward. Forces in these directions combine to hold the club on the correct path into the ball. The forward force primarily comes from the hips sliding laterally toward the target. The major outward force is the torso rotating open, or to the left, and the arms rotating the club over. The downward force results from the right arm straightening and the left arm pulling across the chest. If your swing has too much outward force (rotation) and not enough forward force (slide), you'll swing across the ball, causing pulls and slices. If your swing has too much forward force, you'll swing too much from the inside, causing pushes and hooks. The correct blend of these three forces ensures proper impact.

↑ From the downtarget view, the hands should pass through the body on the downswing at the middle to the top of the right biceps.

↑ **Champion golfers who show the left arm staying in on the downswing. This allows the player to swing outward to the ball and avoid cutting across it.**

Let's look at how the three main pieces of the downswing—the hip and leg action, the spine tilt, and the arm swing—contribute to a powerful and consistent delivery of the club. Then we'll put them together and see how they influence each other as you swing down and through to the finish.

THE HIP AND LEG ACTION

One of the main differences between good and poor players is how fast the hips and legs transfer the weight toward the target. At the start of the downswing, most average golfers get the rotary part right, unwinding their shoulders, but they don't have enough lateral motion toward the target. When the rotary takes over, it not only pushes the club outside the correct arc, leading to shorts that curve to the right, it also positions the swing's low point behind the ball, producing fat or thin contact. The goal is to keep the club on the same swing arc it traced on the backswing as the hip center shifts in front of the ball, setting up a downward and outward strike. Moving the hips toward the target causes the spine to tilt to the golfer's right; this move must be combined with a gradual extension of the spine out of its forward tilt toward the ball—just like on the backswing. The combination of these spine actions keeps the golfer at the same level to the ground, setting up a precise return of the club to the ball.

To start the hips and legs correctly on the downswing, you must immediately lean into your left leg. This shifts more weight to your front side and starts your hips moving toward the target. Your right leg starts to regain its flex and your left leg stays flexed and moves forward as a result of this forward hip slide. As your hips continue to move forward, your left hip gets higher than your right—the opposite of the backswing—and your left leg starts to straighten. The flex in your right knee will be put to good use later, providing leverage for pushing off the ground.

The knee action on the downswing is critical. Here we'll track the shifting of the left knee toward the target and the straightening of both knees. When your left arm reaches parallel to the ground on the downswing (halfway down), your hips have slid about an inch toward the target compared to the top of the backswing, putting your weight 70/30 on the left side. Your left knee has moved an inch in front of your left ankle, as a result of the lateral motion.

When the shaft parallels the ground, your hips have moved another inch toward the target, and your left knee is now two inches in front of your left ankle. Your weight is now 80/20 on the left. At impact, your hips have shifted another inch toward the target, with 90 percent of your weight on your left side. And by the time your right arm is parallel to the ground after impact (halfway through), your weight is 95/5 and the lateral hip slide is complete. The popular advice to make a slight "bump" toward the target with the hips does not transfer enough weight to the left side soon enough or for long

What it feels like: impact

TOMMY ARMOUR III

If you stay forward, you have a lot of leverage when you come into impact. When I'm doing it right, it feels like the ball isn't even there when I hit it. It's a very strong impact, never harsh or clanky, but it's smooth, too. You're really compressing the ball, so it's powerful, but without a lot of effort.

↑ **The left knee stays flexed as weight moves forward on the downswing. Many amateurs straighten the left leg too soon.**

enough. A full sliding of the hips sets the stage for a powerful downswing and ball-first contact.

Pushing your hips forward also starts to release your spine from its left-tilting backswing position on its way to a right-tilting position through impact (face-on view). But your shoulder center should not move; your spine will tilt to the right because your hips are sliding toward the target. This hip action will help create the optimum descent of the club into the ball. How? The forward thrust of the lower body keeps the hands and club to the inside, approaching on a circular arc to the ball, not steeply as they do when the body rotates without sufficient lateral motion. The club is still descending at impact, just not as much as it would be if the hips didn't slide forward.

Think back to how the hips turned on the backswing: on a tilted downward angle, with the right hip moving up and behind you. This angle allows a bigger hip turn and, therefore, a bigger shoulder turn. On the downswing, your hips must release from that tilted angle and level out, because their capacity to turn forward on an angle is limited.

The Stack and Tilt Swing

What it feels like: hip slide

CHARLIE WI

I sometimes practice with a club across my toes and try to slide my hips along that line on the downswing. Golfers have already been taught to turn the hips through the shot, so the key is making the hips go forward for as long as possible.

To level out the hips, you need to push up with your legs, as if you were launching yourself off the ground. Imagine a shot-putter on the release or a tennis player serving: They literally jump off the ground. Your right leg, which has regained its original flex early in the downswing, is now in position to lead this upward thrust. Of course, your feet won't actually leave the ground, but your hips will release from their downward tilt so they can keep turning through the shot.

↑ Golf legends demonstrate the motion of the left knee. Notice how at impact and in the finish, the knee is still in front of the left ankle.

Hip rotation is important for a couple of reasons. Just like on the backswing, more hip turn promotes more shoulder turn. When the hips keep turning, you can maintain your wrist hinge coming down, with the clubhead lagging behind and poised to flash into the ball. The key to an aggressive and continuous hip turn is releasing the hips from their downward tilt, and that's what the upward thrust from the legs does.

The hips must keep turning *and* moving forward because hip rotation alone would keep the body in its forward flex set at address and thereby limit the shoulder turn. Any restriction of hip turn inhibits the forward rotation of the shoulders, which often causes the shoulder center to shift or the shoulders to move onto a more level plane. Both of these changes adversely affect the speed and descent of the club into impact.

The upward thrust of the lower body is another trademark move of Stack & Tilt. This jumping up should start when the club approaches impact (technically, when it reaches parallel to the ground on the downswing). Our experience is that better players often make this move instinctively, because the club is dropping and gaining dynamic weight. To "lighten" the club and avoid a crash into the ground, the good player will push up with his legs as the club nears impact. Less experienced golfers have to consciously "jump" to deliver the club correctly.

What it feels like: hip slide

AARON BADDELEY

I've worked a lot on keeping my tailbone moving forward on the downswing. For me the best image of this is getting my right hip pocket in front of the ball at impact. Of course, the swing is happening so fast that you can't really judge this when you're hitting the ball, but the thought that I'm doing it keeps my hips moving forward.

Along with the feeling of jumping up, another helpful image, as we've discussed, is tucking the butt under the torso through impact. As the legs straighten and push up, the muscles in your rear end should push toward the target, moving the hip center farther forward. This shifts your hips as far as they can go and raises your belt-line three to four inches higher than it was at address, with your tailbone over the inside of your left foot from the face-on view. Tucking the butt creates the Stack & Tilt release: a complete forward and upward thrusting of the hips.

↓ In the Stack & Tilt follow-through, the spine is fully extended (below, left), but the player has stayed in the same tilt toward the ground (below, right). This is possible only when the hips slide forward.

THE SPINE TILT

On the backswing, your spine tilted 35 degrees to the left (which became your forward tilt toward the ball) and stretched out as far as possible. The purpose of these spine actions is to let the upper body turn back without the shoulder center moving off the ball. Coming down, the spine must reverse these positions, with the goal again being to keep the shoulder center in place. If you're getting the feeling that a fixed shoulder center is the biggest priority in the swing, you're starting to understand Stack & Tilt.

To reverse its backswing actions, your spine must start to tilt to the right immediately from the top. The lateral sliding of your hips in conjunction with the unwinding of the shoulders is what allows that to happen: When your hips shift forward and your shoulder center stays, the spine will tilt to the right. When you get halfway down, your spine should be vertical from the face-on view, as it was at address. By impact, your spine should be tilted away from the target, the exact amount depending on how much you shift your hips forward—the wider the stance (and the longer the club), the more your hips slide.

Your spine will continue to tilt farther and farther away from the target until your right arm parallels the ground after impact, when the hip slide is complete. The spine retains that same right tilt to the finish. So the spine tilt you see at impact from the face-on view is the same right tilt you see from downtarget in the finish—it's just turned 90 degrees toward the target because your body has continued to rotate. And you guessed it, the shoulder center has not moved.

Your shoulders retrace their backswing turn on the same steep downward angle all the way through the swing. But the rate of the shoulder turn slows down as the club gets closer to impact, which allows the club to "turn the corner" into the ball. This is your body's natural braking mechanism: The brain senses that if the shoulders kept up their rotational speed, the club would be thrown outside the proper swing arc. In effect, the club has to catch up, so the shoulders—the innermost moving part of the swing—have to brake to allow the arms to extend and the wrists to unhinge. This sends the clubhead—the outermost part—down to the ball. To conform to this principle we like the golfer's shoulders to be square at impact instead of open. When the shoulders spin open, the spine straightens too early and the butt of the club rises, causing excessively pushed shots that often curve farther to the right.

Now for the other spine action: reversing the straightening of the spine on the backswing. In short, your spine must go from flexed forward at address to fully elongated at the top to flexed forward again on the downswing to fully elongated at the finish. This movement has been called the signature move of great golfers by biomechanics experts. On the downswing, the golfer moves back into his forward flexion toward the ball as the right knee flexes back to its original angle. This is the golfer contracting the spine and preparing to jump off the ground to propel the shaft into impact. The dynamic weight of the speeding club will signal the golfer to pull the spine out of its forward flexion. When the club gets roughly three-quarters of the way down, the spine will be in its original forward tilt; this is where experienced golfers have learned to respond to the club's increased dynamic weight and stretch out the spine, catapulting the club into the ball. The millisecond before impact is the only time the spine is in the same forward tilt it held at address. But this is not a conscious move: The weight of the swinging club pulls the spine into that forward tilt and back out of it again, on its way to a full stretch again at the finish.

This stretching of the spine in the follow-through is a result of the lower body pushing forward as the head stays in place. Keeping the top of your spine in place eliminates the need for you to find the right spine position at impact. Look at it this way: The spine tilts left and

---

↓ Varying degrees of spine extension: We prescribe the position in the second frame. The longest hitter is on the left, the shortest on the right.

elongates on the backswing, then tilts right and elongates through impact—but the top of the spine never moves. If you get this right, you'll be on your way to becoming a precise and powerful ball-striker.

These actions of the spine from setup to finish also contribute greatly to power production, literally catapulting the shaft. With the spine wound up and stretched on the backswing, a tremendous amount of energy is stored. Coming down, the golfer uses the forward tilt of the body toward the ball and bend in the knees as powerful levers against the ground. When your spine extends through impact, the top of the spine staying in place, and your knees straighten, maximum energy is transferred—the club is slung into the ball. Picture the speed of a slingshot when the base stays in place; if the base moves with the forward motion, the speed diminishes. Similarly, the weakest way to swing a golf club would be by moving your shoulder center forward through impact, with your spine tilting toward the target and your upper body over your front foot, as many golfers are taught. The familiar hitch in basketball star Charles Barkley's downswing shows a golfer who has not been taught to stand up through the ball.

THE ARM SWING

As your hips slide forward and your spine begins reversing its backswing positions, your arms provide the downward force required to return the club to the ball. First, your left arm begins to pull away from your right shoulder so your right arm can start straightening when the club is halfway down. From this point, your right arm extends continuously until it reaches straight a few feet past impact. To be precise, your right arm should be straight when the shaft is 45 degrees to the ground in the follow-through, not before. High-handicappers tend to straighten the right arm too quickly, which causes the radius of the swing to get too long too fast and the swing's low point to shift behind the ball.

Among better players, a common problem is the arm not pulling away from the right shoulder fast enough. If your hands don't start moving downward from the start, you'll tend to drop your right shoulder to get the club down to the ball. The subconscious mind is very sharp: It will help you find the ball at impact. If the swing radius feels too short because your right arm isn't straightening fast enough, your brain will tell your right shoulder to drop. The problem with that is that it shifts the shoulder center back. Slow-motion video is the best way to track the left arm pulling away from the shoulder and the right arm straightening, which should be gradual and continuous through impact. If your head is falling back on the downswing, it's a good bet your hands are not pulling away from your right shoulder fast enough.

Your hands should start down on the same plane they traced on the backswing. Here's a good checkpoint for the correct path of your hands as the club continues down. Picture the downswing from the downtarget view: When the hands pass through your body, they should be at the middle to the base of your right biceps, just as they were at that point in the backswing. This proves that your hands have stayed on the correct circular arc around the body.

One of the other factors that influences shot direction is the angle of the shaft to the ground at impact from the face-on view. At address the shaft was leaning 5 to 10 degrees toward the target, and that's where it should be at impact for a straight shot. If the butt end of the club moves farther ahead, leaning the shaft more forward, the clubhead will swing more out to the ball, promoting a bigger right-to-left

---

↓ **Tony Lema is a good model for the transition. Notice how his right knee regains its original flex so it can push off the ground.**

The Downswing and Follow-through

curve. If the butt end drops back, so that the shaft is more vertical or even leaning away from the target at impact, the club will swing from out to in, promoting a left-to-right shot.

The forward lean of the shaft also affects where the club hits the ground. We've been saying all along that the location of the weight determines the swing's low point, but the shaft lean also plays a part. The forward lean of the shaft is largely a function of the side angles in the wrists, which should not change during the swing. If the angle between the right arm and the shaft contracts coming into impact, the grip pushes ahead and the low point moves forward. The opposite happens if the angle between the right arm and the shaft increases: The grip falls back and the low point moves back. If you freeze those side angles in your wrists during the swing, the only determinant of the low point is the location of the weight.

→ **The angle established at setup between the right arm and the shaft should remain intact through impact.**

The unhinging of your wrists on the downswing is a result of the club gaining dynamic weight and your right arm straightening, both of which exert a strong outward force and cause the wrists to unhinge. You don't have to consciously unhinge your wrists, and you especially don't want your wrists unhinging too early, which usually means you're hitting at the ball with your hands or your hips are not moving forward fast enough. If your hips slow down, the club will release, and your wrists will unhinge prematurely, causing the club to bottom out behind the ball or cut across it from the outside.

The Stack and Tilt Swing

Let's assume your wrist hinge is the baseline 90 degrees at the top; it should be about 80 degrees when your left arm parallels the ground coming down—it actually increases. Compare this extra loading of the wrists to the cracking of a whip: When the handle goes forward, the tip lags behind and stores more energy. By the time the shaft parallels the ground, the unhinging is well under way, and your wrists should return to their address hinge at impact. From there, your wrists start to rehinge the club, eventually reaching a 90-degree angle with the right arm on the follow-through.

Rehinging is an important action that better players often do instinctively but that less experienced golfers need to focus on. Just as the club got heavy on the downswing, causing your wrists to unhinge, it should still feel heavy after impact, so your wrists rehinge to absorb this force. Rehinging also helps to slow down the club after impact. If your body is left to brake the swing without help from the rehinging of your wrists, the club's momentum can pull you off balance. If you leave it to your arms to brake the swing, the club will wrap around your body, often bouncing harshly off your back—a move that looks powerful but is unnecessary. To encourage rehinging we often tell students to stop the follow-through faster while keeping their arms straight.

What it feels like: rehinging the club

ERIC AXLEY

I hit a lot of practice balls holding tees under my arms. This helps me keep my arms connected to my body as I swing back and through. Especially on the follow-through, if I squeeze my armpits and hold those tees in place, my arms don't fly off my body. This causes my wrists to rehinge to slow down the club. It's a shorter, tighter finish position. I even play practice rounds with tees stuck under my arms. It's a great drill for me—I only wish I could use them in tournaments, too.

The direction of the swing after impact should mirror that of the downswing, with the hands and arms staying on the same around-the-body arc. When your right arm reaches parallel to the ground after impact (halfway through), it should be angled well inside the target line, not pointing straight out at the target. This is a mirror image of your left arm at parallel on the downswing, and proves that the club has stayed on its arc without any manipulation by the hands or arms. It also shows that your body has kept up its rotational speed, allowing the club to swing around your body as it moves through impact.

As the club continues into the follow-through, it should start tracking upward. A good checkpoint here is from the downtarget view: Where does the club reappear out of the left side of the body? It should pass through your body at the middle to top of your left biceps. When the club swings too vertically after impact, the shaft will reappear at the neck or even the head. This is a position we check constantly with our students, because it shows how the club moved through the shot. In fact, trying to swing the club below the left shoulder can be a quick fix for players who get too vertical in the follow-through and tend to hook the ball.

↑ Compare pulls (left two photos) to pushes (right two photos). Notice how the club reappears below the left shoulder and the shoulders are turned more for the pull.

The Stack and Tilt Swing

Your arms should stay extended through impact, but make sure to keep them soft enough to flex slightly and absorb the final bit of speed. If your wrists and arms function in these ways after impact, there is no need for the classic wraparound finish. The follow-through should be short and crisp, not long and loose with the club rebounding off your back.

Keeping your arms extended also helps you swing outward longer and hit the ground. When your arms flex through impact, the club tends to miss the ground completely and the path tends to be across the ball from out to in. Remember, the shoulders are turning in a circle with the center staying in place; if the arms flex, it changes the distance the club is to the ground, which leads to erratic contact. Straight arms is also one of the major pieces that separate players who draw the ball from those who slice it.

Let's backtrack for a moment and take a snapshot at impact from both the face-on and downtarget views. From face-on, your spine is tilted slightly away from the target, because your hips have slid forward several inches (the exact amount depends on the club). With a middle iron, your left knee should be two inches forward of your left ankle. Your weight should be 90/10 on your front foot, and the shaft should be at the same angle to the ground as it was at address, with your right arm almost extended. Both legs are essentially straight, pushing upward, with your left hip higher than your right. The head and shoulder center are precisely where they were at address.

→ **Stack & Tilt impact: The hips push forward, tilting the spine away from the target without the head moving back.**

From the downtarget view, your spine is in its original forward tilt toward the ball, putting you at the same height as you were at setup. Your shoulders are square, facing the ball, and your hips are turned open 30 to 45 degrees. The shaft is at the same angle to the ground as it was in the address position, pointing at the top of your zipper. Your rear end is flexed upward, tucking under your torso. Practice posing these impact alignments, and check your positions in a mirror or on video. Getting a feel for where you should be at impact will be helpful when you try to reach these positions at full speed.

⬃ From the downtarget view, the shoulders are square and the shaft is at the same angle to the ground as it was in the setup.

THE DOWNSWING IN SEQUENCE

Now that we've explained the moves and positions that constitute the downswing and through-swing, let's consider them in sequence. Remember, the downswing is a blend of three forces: forward, outward, and downward. From the top, your hips start to slide laterally (forward force), moving the weight of your lower body continuously to your left side. Your shoulders begin to turn toward the target (out-

The Stack and Tilt Swing

ward force), pulling your left arm away from your right shoulder and lowering your arms (downward force).

When your left arm reaches parallel to the ground, it is angled well inside the target line, from the downtarget view. At this point your right arm begins to straighten and push outward on the shaft, which causes your wrists to start unhinging. Check the angle between your right arm and the shaft from your perspective: It should be what it was at address, proving that minimal independent rotation of the joints in your arms and wrists has occurred.

◤ **Coming down, no rotation of the hands and arms holds the shaft on the correct angle.**

When the club parallels the ground coming down, your hips are still moving laterally, but the shoulder turn has started to slow down relative to the club, which allows the club to "turn the corner" into impact. This slowing down of the shoulders transfers speed to your arms and then the club. This is a major element that experienced players use to accelerate the club into impact, like cracking a whip, known in instruction circles as the kinetic sequence. Your shoulders are essentially square at impact, while your hips are 30 to 45 degrees open and still pushing forward, aided by the upward thrusting of your legs. If your hips stop moving toward the target, your spine will stop tilting to the right and the shaft will kick to the outside, putting the swing path across the ball. Remember, the forward motion of your hips is what keeps the club on the proper inside path. If the rotary motion outpaces the lateral motion, the club is thrown to the outside.

At impact, your right arm is still straightening and will not be completely straight until the club is well into the follow-through. Your wrists are back to their original hinge at impact, but they do not roll over, as many golfers believe. Your hips continue to press forward and turn, and your shoulder center stays in place, causing your spine to flex away from the target. Again, if your hips stop moving laterally, the momentum of the club will take over and flip the club-head past your hands, shifting the low point behind the ball and causing the club to cut across it.

When your right arm is parallel to the ground after impact, it is angled well inside the target line, just as your left arm was in the corresponding position in the downswing. At this point your brain knows that the speed of the club must be absorbed, so the wrists start rehinging. Your right arm stays straight well into the follow-through, maintaining the width of the swing. If you don't push up with your legs quickly enough, your elbows pull apart, causing a "chicken wing" finish with the elbows flexing outward.

What it feels like: straight arms

MIKE WEIR

The idea of keeping my arms straight through impact was different for me because I never had much extension through the ball. But when I kept my arms long, I hit the ball stronger and straighter. The feeling for me was that my arms stayed straight for a long time through the shot, like I was hitting a really long punch shot. It felt strange, but then I'd look on video and see that my arms were perfect.

The Stack and Tilt Swing

It is important to have a clearly defined finish position, because your brain won't let you swing the club as fast as you can without knowing you can handle the speed and stay in balance. At the finish, your hips are as far forward as they can go, your spine is fully stretched away from the target, your left leg is straight and your right is straighter than it was at address, and your wrists are fully re-hinged. A good indicator that your hips have moved forward and rotated properly is the position of your right foot at the finish: It should be angled 45 degrees inward, away from the target line, not fully up on its toes. And no space should be visible between your knees from the downtarget view.

← **The Stack & Tilt finish: We tell students to swing harder but stop faster than the conventional wraparound finish.**

THE POWER PACKAGE

Hitting the ball a long way is what average golfers want most, but being able to create power and also exhibit a predictable shot pattern will help your game much more. Many golfers think inconsistency is an unavoidable side effect of increasing power. To an extent that is true, because some moves that allow a player to swing faster reduce precision. But almost anyone can learn to hit the ball farther and at the same time develop more control. Let's look at how power is generated in the Stack & Tilt Swing.

Two major power factors are often overlooked. First, hitting the ball with the middle of the clubface is a prerequisite to maximizing ball speed off the club. Any method that compromises center-face contact for more speed is inefficient. Second, using the loft on the clubface effectively determines how high the ball will fly and, therefore, how far it will go. If the loft on the face is increased at impact—we call this using positive loft—distance is often reduced. If the loft is decreased—negative loft—trajectory and carry get to the point of diminishing returns with the lower-lofted clubs.

Good players tend to hit shorter clubs with negative loft, and longer clubs with positive loft. The 8-iron might have 40 degrees of loft on the clubface, but at impact the tour player might launch it at 35 degrees; with a 9-degree driver, the tour player's launch angle might be 10 or 12 degrees. Why use negative loft with the shorter clubs?

The answer is backspin. Better players know that by playing the ball back in their stance they can hit a lower shot that spins more for added control.

For longer shots, this low launch with high spin is not ideal because spin reduces control in the longer clubs. Experienced players use positive loft with the driver and fairway woods by moving the ball forward and widening the stance. This positions the low point closer to the ball (not as far in front of it) and increases the loft potential. However, playing the ball farther forward elevates the risk of swinging across it and hitting a slice. To combat this, the player must increase the hip slide on the downswing to keep the club swinging from the inside. Less-experienced players, who might struggle to move the hips forward enough, should push their hips farther forward at address.

What it feels like: arm swing

DEAN WILSON

Because I used to swing my arms so far out and up on the backswing, when Andy and Mike put my arms in the correct position at the top, it actually felt like I was swinging my left arm around my beltline! They would take a picture of this position, then show it to me, and I couldn't believe it: It was in perfect position. My feel was way off, but their geometry wasn't. It felt foreign at first, but my ball-striking told me I was on the right track.

It's worth noting here why a few of the methods commonly used to increase loft on the driver for a higher launch don't work. Some golfers tip the spine away from the target at address, but that makes it difficult to tilt the spine left on the backswing, as our method prescribes. Plus, too much tilt to the right on the downswing often leads to the clubface closing too fast through the ball. Other players lean the shaft away from the target at address, but that actually closes the clubface from the start and increases the chances of swinging across the ball and hitting a slice. The popular belief that keeping the hands ahead of the ball decreases loft is not necessarily true. When the hands stay in front, the club can swing from the inside and hit with a more lofted face. In fact, the highest draws are produced with the butt end of the grip the farthest forward and the face the most open. Teeing the ball higher is another common piece of advice for increasing launch angle. But the problem there is, just like with tipping the spine to the right at address, you'll struggle to hit solid shots with a square clubface.

In the last few years on tour we've seen some of the traditional power moves disappear. Players are teeing the ball lower and swinging their hands more to the inside. They're also staying more on top of the ball, with less tilt to the right on the backswing. These moves can be seen in great players of the past; we're not taking credit for them. In fact, many of the best players in history have straightened their right knee on the backswing to facilitate hip turn—another move we're seeing more and more on tour. Remember, swinging inward and stretching the spine on the backswing and again through impact to catapult the shaft are the lowest common denominators in creating power. Just look at the longest drivers, and you'll see.

Let's review how the Stack & Tilt Swing maximizes clubhead speed. First, when the hands and club stay to the inside, you access the speed of the circular arc. The more inward and upward the hands go without lifting off the rib cage or causing the shoulder center to shift, the more power they can generate.

Second, the spine tilt (to the left going back and to the right coming down) keeps the shoulder center stable, which allows the clubhead to swing from a stable axis and, therefore, move faster. In effect you use your body as a platform to sling the shaft by alternately flexing and straightening your spine as we've described. These spine actions also increase the range of motion in your hips and shoulders, which boosts rotational speed and power.

↑ **The change in the spine angle from forward flex to full extension acts as a giant power lever, catapulting the shaft through the ball.**

Third, the braking of your shoulders and hands before impact serves to transfer more speed to the clubhead. Picture again the cracking of a whip: The handle accelerates quickly but then stops, sending speed out to the tip. The power of the body turn in the golf swing supplies significant power, but your body's braking system allows the levers in the arms and wrists to unload, multiplying that power. Your wrists unhinge through impact; your left arm pulls down across your chest; and your right arm straightens. These levers must be fully utilized to maximize clubhead speed.

The Downswing and Follow-through

5

STACK & TILT VERSUS THE CONVENTIONAL SWING

DEAN WILSON

I first met Andy and Mike in the middle of the 2004 season. My golf game was at an all-time low, especially my ball-striking. At the time I was focusing on shifting my weight to the right side on the backswing while keeping the clubhead outside of my hands. This caused my arms to disconnect from my body, which made it tough to hit the ball consistently. I was hitting as many balls on the range as my body and daylight would permit, in hopes of finding a key that would get me through the next day's round. But by ingraining all those bad habits I was only digging myself a deeper hole.

Luckily I was introduced to Andy and Mike, and with their help I was able to see light at the end of the tunnel. What I liked the most about their system was that they had measured all the swings of the game's greatest players and were able to show me how they worked. They knew how to explain it and how to map it out, and when I started trying the different pieces, I knew they were right.

They helped me lower my arms by a good 20 degrees going back, and steepen the angle of my shoulders 10 degrees while staying centered. This got me to where my backswing plane was consistent with all the clubs in the bag, and in turn I saw instant results on the course. Two weeks after first working with Andy and Mike I had my best finish of the year, and over the next ten events I continually improved my ball-striking.

With their help I was able to explain my misses and to correct them in the middle of a round. Because my swing has always tended to be long and loose, we've tried to make it more compact by getting my shoulders to brake on the downswing so that my wrists can recock the club for a quicker, crisper action. For a visual example of this, I love to watch Aaron Baddeley and Tommy Armour hit balls. Their swings are very short, compact, and crisp and have a lot of speed.

Many average golfers struggle to play at a decent level for two reasons: (1) bad information and (2) misinterpretation of information. Go to any golf course or driving range and you'll hear all kinds of clichés used to explain bad shots. Things like "I got quick" or "I didn't release it" or "I lost my balance." Some explanations like these are just plain wrong, while others may identify a problem, but the solution chosen does not address the real issue.

An example of bad information is the weight shift. Players have long been told to shift to the right foot on the backswing so they can drive into the ball on the downswing. But the shift-right model is too unpredictable, especially when practiced by inexperienced players. Plus, as the historical photos in this book show, some of the best and most powerful golfers the game has known never shifted off the ball in the backswing. They might think they did, they might feel like they did, but the pictures prove they did not. The notion that power comes from loading onto the right side is false, and yet it is commonly taught today.

↑ Players have long been told to turn the upper body behind the ball (above, left) but rotating the shoulders in a circle (above, right) keeps you over the ball for predictable contact.

For an example of misinterpretation, consider the term "extension." The idea that the left arm should stay straight going back and the right arm should not collapse into the body is absolutely true. But when the player takes that to mean that he should swing the club straight away from the ball, pushing the arms back and keeping the club "in front of the body," problems arise. That kind of extension pulls the player off the ball and causes the arms to lift off the rib cage—two of the primary faults that lead to swinging across the ball. We measure extension by how straight the arms are as they swing inward on a circular arc. That's no less extended than the straightaway swing, it's just conforming to the principle of swinging in a circle. So extension is important, yes, but the wrong kind of extension is disastrous.

↑ **We measure the player's backswing width by how far inward the hands go, not by how far they extend straight back away from the ball.**

The Stack and Tilt Swing

The speed of the swing is another concept used as a crutch by a lot of golfers. They hit a poor shot and say, "I swung too fast." Well, swinging the clubhead at a high speed and in rhythm is one of the marks of the good player's swing. We'd be the first to say that good rhythm is critical to allowing the pieces of the swing to play out in the proper sequence, but it's not a cure-all for poor mechanics. It's certainly not the "glue that holds the swing together," as we've heard players and teachers say.

The correct sequence is critical, not only in the execution of a swing but also in the approach taken to learning the game. Too often we see players working on things in the wrong order. They're hitting a slice, so they strengthen their grip, which might be a problem they have to address, but it's usually not the reason they're slicing. As a result, they end up with a contorted swing made up of Band-Aids with no regard for structural form. The slice is a result of swinging across the ball, so slicers need to move the weight forward, keep the grip end of the club forward, keep the hands in, and so on. A grip change might come later, but it should not be one of the first items on the priority list.

What follows is a comparison of Stack & Tilt to typical positions that result from what is conventionally taught. Of course we look at each student individually, but you can scan your local driving range and see these faults almost to a player. After all, these are the things they've been taught. Here we've isolated the most important mechanical positions at each stage in the swing. You'll see that our positions are very different—often the complete opposite—and you'll see why Stack & Tilt is superior to what most golfers are doing, whether they're doing it because of bad instruction or simple misunderstanding.

Address (6-iron)

CONVENTIONAL

Side tilt

► The spine is tilted away from the target, with the right shoulder down, positioning the head behind the ball. This presets a shift to the right on the backswing, which requires a return shift to the left in time for impact to avoid bottoming out behind the ball.

Weight distribution

► With the hips and shoulders tilted away from the target, more weight is on the back foot, which further encourages a shift off the ball on the takeaway.

Shaft position

► The grip end of the club is pulled back so that it points between the arms.

Stance

► The center of the hips is set over the back half of the stance, well behind the ball.

Posture

► The spine is straight and the shoulders are pulled back (down-target view). The golfer must view the ball out of the bottoms of his eyes, which is awkward, and the stiff, unnatural back and shoulder positions restrict range of motion.

The Stack and Tilt Swing

Side tilt

► From the face-on view, the spine is essentially straight up and down, with the shoulders nearly level and stacked over the hips. This encourages the shoulders to turn in a circle on the backswing, without the upper body shifting behind the ball.

Weight distribution

► The hips are level and pushed slightly toward the target, and the shoulders are almost level—the right shoulder is a touch lower only because the right hand is lower on the grip. The weight favors the front foot 55/45, slightly more for the driver.

Shaft position

► The grip end of the club is forward, opposite the inside of the left leg.

Stance

► The center of the hips is set over the front half of the stance, in line with the ball.

Posture

► The head is down, so the golfer can view the ball easily in his central vision. The back is slightly rounded, in a natural anatomical position, and the shoulders are rolled inward slightly to create pressure points at the armpits that extend nearly halfway down the arms for a feeling of connection between the arms and front of the torso.

CONVENTIONAL

Hand path
► The hands and arms extend the club straight back away from the ball, keeping the club in front of the body and pulling the right arm immediately off the chest.

Shoulder turn
► The left shoulder begins to turn level, lifting the shoulders off the downward angle established at address.

Wrist hinge
► The wrists have not started hinging because the spine is not tilting to the left. The club stays low for the first few feet.

Ascent of the hands
► The hands move level to the ground, the old "low-and-slow takeaway."

Hand path

► The hands immediately start moving back, up, and in, facilitated by the spine tilt to the left.

Shoulder turn

► The left shoulder turns down and in, which helps move the club to the inside and elevates the clubhead off the ground. The shoulders begin turning at a right angle to the forward tilt of the spine at address.

Wrist hinge

► The hands and club ascend at a consistent rate because the wrists are hinging continuously from the start of the swing.

Ascent of the hands

► The hands begin to ascend on an arc, not trace a straight line level to the ground.

Misconception: "Swing the club straight back"

The club should move on a circular arc, tracking to the inside from the start of the swing. When the club moves straight back, the right arm pulls away from the body and the hands tend to lift the club. Extending the club away from the ball also can pull the body away from the target.

CONVENTIONAL

Arm swing

► The arms have run out of extension, so they start to lift the club off the circular arc, disconnecting the upper arms from the chest and pulling the right elbow farther away from the right side.

Wrist hinge

► The wrists have not hinged enough because the right elbow is pulling up and off the rib cage and the hands are not ascending.

Shoulder center

► As the body starts to rotate away from the target, the body's forward tilt is maintained and the top of the spine shifts to the right, moving the shoulder center off the ball.

Weight shift

► With the body moving over the right leg, more weight shifts to the right foot.

Misconception: "Make a level turn"

The torso tilts toward the ball about 35 degrees at address, and the shoulders should rotate at a right angle to that spine tilt throughout the swing. If they pull off that plane and turn level, the shoulder center tends to shift to the right on the backswing, leading to unpredictable contact.

Arm swing
► The arms continue on an inward arc, with the left arm moving across the chest and the right elbow staying close to the right side and flexing to 90 degrees.

Wrist hinge
► The club is moving gradually inward and upward because the wrists are hinging at a constant rate as the shoulders turn.

Shoulder center
► The upper body is rotating in a circle, with the left shoulder continuing to turn downward and inward uniformly. The spine is tilting to the left and extending, which allows the shoulder center to stay in place and the head to stay the same height.

Weight shift
► Like the shoulders, the hips turn in a circle, so no weight shifts to the right foot.

CONVENTIONAL

Spine tilt

► The spine has maintained most of its address tilt, so the upper body has turned behind the ball, moving the shoulder center several inches to the right. The shoulders have made a level turn.

Arm swing

► Continuing on a vertical plane, the arms have nowhere to go but up. When they can't go any higher, they flex more and the wrists collapse and drop the club toward the head. The right arm also breaks down and flexes away from the body.

Leg action

► The left knee moves inward, toward the right, and the knees do not change from their address flex.

Hip turn

► The hip rotation is severely limited because the right knee stays flexed. The hips are turning level, or the left hip is higher than the right.

Misconception: "Keep the right knee flexed"

Many players think that maintaining the flex in the right knee established at address stabilizes the lower body and prevents the hips from turning more on the backswing. That last part is true, but most golfers need more hip turn, not less. Straightening the right leg can double the amount your hips rotate, and more hip turn means more shoulder turn. So forget about keeping that flex.

Spine tilt

► To keep the shoulder center steady, the spine continues to tilt to the left and extend. This also allows the head to stay at the same height it was at address; in effect, the left tilt becomes the tilt toward the ball when the body rotates 90 degrees.

Arm swing

► The hands and arms continue on a consistent inward arc, putting the hands several inches behind the right shoulder at the top (downtarget view). The arm swing appears shorter and more compact because the left arm has stayed on the chest, and the right elbow has stayed close to the right side.

Leg action

► The right knee has straightened and the left knee has flexed forward, toward the ball.

Hip turn

► The straightening and flexing of the legs allows the hips to turn freely, with the right hip moving up and back. The hips are turning on the same downward angle they held at address.

Halfway down (left arm parallel to the ground)

CONVENTIONAL

Weight shift

►After a small forward shift, if any, to start the downswing, the weight remains largely on the right foot, and the head is behind the ball.

Hip action

►The hips, which made a level turn going back, now reverse direction, spinning open without making a significant lateral move toward the target.

Hand path

►With the hips and shoulders turning and inadequate hip slide, the hands and arms are pulled outside the correct downswing path. Good players compensate by standing up sooner to try to drop the shaft, but higher-handicappers tend to hit pulls and slices.

Clubhead lag

►The right arm straightens too soon and releases the wrist hinge, so clubhead lag is lost. Then the arms start to roll over and move the club on an outside path. The club quickly gets heavy, dissipating any remaining wrist hinge.

Weight shift

► From the top, more weight continually moves into the front side, creating downward pressure in the left leg. When the left arm parallels the ground, 70 percent of the weight is left. The head is still in its address position, over the ball (face-on view).

Hip action

► The hips start sliding toward the target as soon as the downswing begins, and then gradually start rotating to the left.

Hand path

► The lateral hip slide helps keep the hands to the inside, retracing their backswing arc on the way down to the ball.

Clubhead lag

► The wrists, which hinged fully on the backswing, remain loaded as the hips move toward the target. The club stays to the inside, so there is no need to roll the wrists and elbows. The lag is preserved.

CONVENTIONAL

Lower-body action
►The lower body provides little leverage or power at impact, because there is no spring in the knees or forward thrust from the hips.

Swing path
►The club swings through impact on an out-to-in path, cutting across the ball and typically causing fades or slices.

Face angle
►The clubface is open to the swing path because the club cut across the ball, so the face makes glancing contact, imparting slice spin and increasing the loft at impact. The ball will curve to the right.

Low point
►With the weight back, the swing reaches its low point behind the ball, causing either a fat shot or thin contact on the upswing.

Lower-body action

► The hips continue to slide laterally as the legs push upward, releasing the hips from their forward tilt and allowing them to turn through impact.

Swing path

► The club strikes the ball as it completes its outward arc from the inside, with the wrists unhinging the club into the ball for full power and ball compression.

Face angle

► The clubface is a few degrees open to the target at impact but slightly closed to the swing path, so it imparts draw spin on the ball. The ball will start to the right and curve left, with no conscious rolling of the hands or wrists.

Low point

► With the shoulder center over the ball and the hips pushing forward, the overall swing center is slightly ahead of the ball, so contact comes just before the club bottoms out. The divot starts after impact.

Follow-through (right arm parallel to the ground)

Wrist angles
►The wrists continue to break down and roll over until the right wrist is flat and the left wrist is bent back. This causes the clubhead to pass the handle, flipping the club upward.

Spine extension
►With the shoulders continuing to turn level, the spine tips back, but the absence of any springing action from the legs keeps the upper body short and compacted.

Hip turn
►The hips have not pushed forward, so they spin out weakly, the hip center staying between the feet.

Leg action
►The right knee stays in place, and too much weight remains on the right foot.

Wrist angles

► The angle between the right arm and the shaft and the flat (or almost flat) position of the left wrist have stayed intact through impact. No rolling or flipping of the club has occurred.

Spine extension

► The head has remained in its address position as the hips have slid forward and the legs have pushed upward. This causes the spine to tilt away from the target and fully elongate.

Hip turn

► The rear end is tucked under the upper body, and the hips, released from their downward tilt by the springing of the legs, turn level and face the target. The hip center is over the left foot.

Leg action

► The left leg is straight and the right leg nearly straight. The right knee does not reach the left because the hip center shifts well forward as the right leg straightens.

CONVENTIONAL

Arm position
► The arms are folded on the chest, and the club wraps around the body, bouncing off the back to stop the swing.

Wrist rehinging
► With the wrists rolling and flipping through the hitting area, they do not rehinge the club correctly after impact.

Body rotation
► Because the hands and arms released past the body, the torso stops turning and sags at the finish.

Weight location
► The hips have not pushed forward, so too much weight remains on the back foot.

Misconception: "Release the club"

To most golfers we've asked, the release means rolling the hands and arms over through impact to close the clubface. Well, that move might close the face, but it also causes the clubhead to pass the hands, which puts the club on an out-to-in path. Amateurs try to fix a slice by releasing the club, but they're making their path more across the ball—and their slice worse.

Arm position
► The upward thrusting of the lower body has thrown the arms off the chest. They straighten and extend to the finish.

Wrist rehinging
► Because they have maintained their side angles and unhinged properly down to the ball, the wrists can rehinge to absorb the speed of the swing without the club crashing into the back.

Body rotation
► The hips have turned 80 to 90 degrees toward the target, the shoulders 90 to 110. The torso faces the target or slightly left of it.

Weight location
► The lower body has pushed forward and upward, so only 5 percent of the weight is on the right foot at the finish.

STACK & TILT VERSUS CONVENTIONAL

	STACK & TILT	CONVENTIONAL
POSTURE	Back is curved; head is down.	Back is straight; head is up.
SPINE ANGLE	Continuously changes to keep the shoulders turning in a circle.	Maintains its forward tilt so the player moves behind the ball.
WEIGHT	Forward at address; keeps moving forward to the finish.	Shifts back, then shifts forward but rarely enough.
HAND PATH	Moves in a circular arc around the body.	Extends away from the body on an artificially wide arc.
KNEE FLEX	Back leg straightens on the backswing.	Back leg stays flexed on the backswing.
THROUGH IMPACT	No roll in wrists or arms; clubface stays square to the swing arc.	Wrists and arms roll in an attempt to square the face.
FOLLOW-THROUGH	Hips forward; head still; spine fully stretched.	Hips back; upper body short and compacted.
BALL FLIGHT	Concept: Clubface controls starting line; swing path controls curve.	Concept: Swing path controls starting line; clubface controls curve.

6

CIRCLES AND CONES

CHARLIE WI

When I first hit balls with Andy and Mike, at the Hartford event in August 2005, I didn't really know where my shots were going. It was my first year on tour, and I would hit a pull, then a cut, then a pull-draw, and so on. The way they explained what was happening in my swing, and what I should try to do, made sense. I told them I was going to empty my head, so give it all to me. I was ready to make changes.

The first thing they told me to do was to keep my center on the ball, instead of shifting to the right on the backswing. At first when I tried it, I felt like I was going eight inches in front of the ball. But I could see the difference in my ball-striking right away. Before that, I never really knew what was going on at impact, so understanding the cause and effect was huge.

I started playing with Stack & Tilt right away, and three weeks after that first session in Hartford, I shot 65 at the 84 Lumber Classic and led after the first day. I finally knew where the ball was going. And when it didn't go where I wanted it to, I knew why.

With my old swing, if I took a week off and didn't hit balls, I felt like I was starting over when I came back. Now I can take time off and pick up where I left off, because I know what my priorities are. I hit the ball a lot straighter, but even more important, I get what's happening in my swing.

Now that we've discussed the major pieces of the Stack & Tilt Swing, you need to understand how the club and ball interact at impact to produce certain shots. This is where our experience with tour players really comes into play. The pros are already hitting the ball solidly and generating sufficient power—our first two fundamentals. They want to groove a more playable, more repeatable ball flight, which is our third fundamental. That's what this chapter is about.

One of the main goals of the better player is to "eliminate half of the golf course," or to develop a shot pattern that restricts misses to one side. Traditional instruction says that the draw eliminates misses to the right and the fade eliminates misses to the left. We teach the opposite, because the worst miss for any golfer is the one that curves across the target, or curves too much—the draw that draws too much or the fade that fades too much. These are the most difficult shots to control and the quickest to turn into severe misses, and they should, therefore, be strictly avoided.

We teach that the only acceptable misses for the player who draws the ball are a push or a draw that doesn't curve all the way to the target. Likewise for the fader, the only good misses are a pull or a fade that doesn't curve as much as expected. The over-curve, as we call it, that moves across the target creates too wide a shot pattern for the player to be effective. Everything we do with players who move the ball left or right is to try to prevent over-curves.

TWO SOCIETIES OF BALL-STRIKERS

Imagine the swing path as a circular arc painted on the ground to represent the path the club takes swinging back and then through the ball. Now picture a straight line from the ball to the target; this is the target line. The point where the line touches the circle is the point of tangency. Mathematically speaking, the perfect swing is when the club traces the circular arc and contacts the ball just before the point of tangency and the ball separates from the clubface a split second later right at the point. If the clubface is square to the target when the ball leaves the face, the shot will start straight and stay straight. That's because the face is square to both the target and the swing path.

↑ **Impact on pushes comes on the back side of the arc, with the club swinging outward; impact on pulls and fades comes on the front side, with the club swinging across the ball.**

All golfers can be split into two groups as it relates to this diagram: those who strike the ball on the back side of the circle, with the clubhead still swinging outward, and those who make contact on the front side, with the clubhead having reached its apex and returning to the inside, swinging across the ball. To find out which group you belong to, look at your typical ball flight: If you hit pulls or slices, you're hitting on the front side; if you hit pushes or hooks, you're hitting on the back side.

→ **Weight forward and handle forward for a draw (left). Weight back and handle back for a fade (right).**

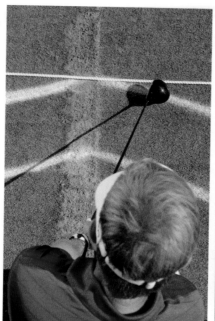

Throughout the history of golf you can find great players who hit on the back side and great players who hit on the front side—although those who hit on the back side make up the majority of tour pros and better golfers. For players who draw the ball, the clubface is pointing right of the target at impact, causing the ball to start to the right, but pointing left of the swing path, causing it to curve left—the classic draw.

Players who hit on the front side of the circle tend to start the ball to the left and curve it right. Shots that start straight and curve to the right also are indicative of this pattern. Many average golfers curve the ball left to right, often out of necessity and excessively so because of faults in their technique, although many good players have acquired a way to use this shot effectively. In this case, the clubface is pointing left of the target at impact, causing the ball to start left, but pointing right of the swing path, causing it to curve right—the classic fade.

What causes contact to be on the back or front side of the circle? Three conditions: 1) ball position, 2) the location of the weight, and 3) the angle of the shaft at impact. This assumes that your hands have continued to swing on their circular arc, without moving outside or farther inside. If your hands stay on the arc, these are the only three factors that determine where the club hits on the circle.

Let's look at a couple of examples of this concept. If the ball position is back, the weight is forward, and the shaft angle is at least at the baseline position (the butt of the club opposite the left thigh), the club will hit on the back side. If the ball position is forward, the weight is back and the butt of the club is pulled back, the club will hit on the front side.

← For the biggest draw, the weight goes forward the farthest and the shaft leans forward the most (left). For the biggest fade, the weight stays back the most and the shaft leans back (right).

If you hit on the back or front side, you might exhibit one of these three conditions, or all three of them. To cause contact the farthest back on the circle, the ball would be back the farthest, the weight would be forward the most, and the shaft would lean forward the most. To cause contact the farthest forward, the ball would be forward the farthest, the weight would be back the most, and the shaft would lean back the most. These positions are not advisable for normal shots, but they do demonstrate the extremes of the circle diagram.

SHOT-CLASSIFICATION SYSTEM

We've discussed how starting direction and curve work together to give a shot its overall direction, so let's look at the various shots they can produce. There are eleven combinations of face and path that create the universe of ball flights, all of which can occur to varying degrees. Here we'll outline them, looking from left to right.

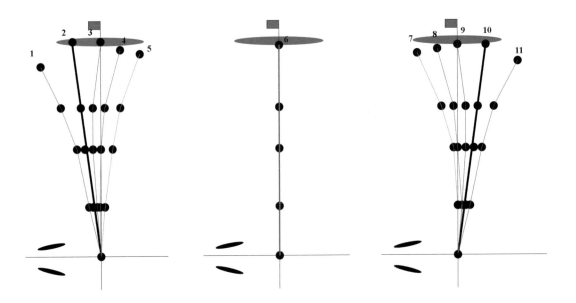

The Stack and Tilt Swing

1 **Pull-hook:** Starts left of the target and curves left.

2 **Pull:** Starts left of or at the target and flies straight.

3 **Fade:** Starts left of the target and curves to it.

4 **Over-fade:** Starts left of or at the target and curves across it.

5 **Slice:** Starts at or right of the target and curves right.

6 **Straight shot:** Starts at the target and flies straight.

7 **Hook:** Starts at or left of the target and curves left.

8 **Over-draw:** Starts right of or at the target and curves across it.

9 **Draw:** Starts right of the target and curves to it.

10 **Push:** Starts right of the target and flies straight.

11 **Push-slice:** Starts right of the target and curves right.

We cannot stress enough the importance of accurately identifying the shots you're hitting, using this naming convention. Reading ball flight tells you everything you need to know about the club's path and face angle at impact. All swing adjustments begin with a precise evaluation of where your shots start and how they curve.

Most golfers, even tour players, have a certain shot they worry about hitting. The problem is, they often misdiagnose the shot; for instance, they call a slice a push or a hook a pull. Players also get the causes wrong. They'll say "I came over the top" when they hit a ball left, but swinging over the top actually causes a slice. Or they'll say "I got ahead of it" when they hit a slice, but having the weight forward promotes a draw. TV commentators use these terms incorrectly, too, so they filter down to the golfing public. Now we have a population of golfers who don't use accurate language.

To identify and name any shot, all you need to know is whether it starts left or right of the target and which way it curves. One way to do this is to lay a long rope on the target line, extending out toward the target, and hit some balls. Shots struck with an open face start right of the rope; those struck with a closed face start left. Or as they relate to our circle diagram: Shots hit on the back side of the circle start right, and those hit on the front side start left.

→ **Use a long rope on the target line to determine starting direction. Shots hit on the front side of the circle with a closed face start to the left.**

It's not always that simple because of one factor: alignment. If your alignment is shifted substantially to the left, you can hit on the back side of the circle and play a fade. Likewise, if your alignment is well right, you can hit on the front side and play a draw. In these cases, you're aligned more in one direction than the clubface is aimed in the other.

Consider Jack Nicklaus's ball flight over the years. Nicklaus often played a push-fade: His alignment was well left, but he hit the ball with an open clubface, so his shots would start right of his stance line but still left of the target, creating room for his fade. He

The Stack and Tilt Swing

was aligned more left than his clubface was aimed right. Other effective push-faders include Lee Trevino, Fred Couples, and Colin Montgomerie.

The push-fade is similar to the draw in that impact is made on the back side of the circle, which makes contact more predictable because the club is still swinging outward, with the low point farther forward. The push-fade is also a longer shot than the pull-fade, because the pull-fader swings across the ball, rolling his wrists and, therefore, throwing away wrist hinge. When the hinge is lost, the distance from the clubhead to the ball in the last part of the downswing is reduced, giving the player less room to accelerate the club. This is why the draw and the push-fade are preferable for power: They preserve wrist hinge and create more room for last-second acceleration into impact.

That said, there have been many successful pull-faders in the game, including Vijay Singh, Bruce Lietzke, Craig Stadler, and Paul Azinger. These players have found ways to make the pull-fade work, but they are at a disadvantage because they have to close the clubface dramatically on the downswing to maintain its relationship with a swing path that is moving across the ball. Most amateurs using this technique have trouble hitting lower-lofted clubs high enough because closing the face that much takes a lot of loft off the shot.

What about the pull-draw, or aiming far enough right to hit a pull that still has room to draw to the target? It's harder to find top-level players who hit a pull-draw, but there are some notable examples, including Arnold Palmer and Sam Snead. The pull-draw is a strong, hard-running shot, which makes it tougher to control on today's firm and fast courses. Highly adapted players who use this technique on some shots change it on others, consciously or subconsciously, to avoid the shot's consequences. This hightlights why you can't just emulate pictures of great players without knowing what shot they were trying to hit: You can find pictures of any great player making all kinds of swings.

Let's look at the three most preferred ball flights—the draw, the straight shot, and the fade—and leave the other shots for Chapter 8, "Fixing Common Faults." Once you know the shot you want to play, start by taking your grip and setting the club to the ball in a way that promotes that shot. We call this creating an "attachment" at address.

UNDERSTANDING ATTACHMENTS

The attachment comprises three setup elements: (1) the angle of the clubface, (2) the height of the butt of the club, and its change from setup to impact, if any, and (3) the placement of the hands on the grip. Logically, there are three types of attachments—closed, square, and open—to match the three basic ball flights—fade, straight, and draw.

We recommend developing a draw or straight shot, but there are times when hitting a fade is preferable. Not only does every player encounter situations that call for a left-to-right shot, but the lower trajectory of the pull-fade can be useful in certain conditions, such as hitting into a headwind or under tree branches. Moreover, many professionals have had successful careers playing the pull-fade, so it certainly merits a place in our system.

To promote your desired ball flight, you have to adjust the attachment at address. We're hesitant to change hand rotation on the club because that's the least important of the three attachment elements in influencing a shot's curve. In addition, if you're like most players, you probably don't want to change your grip. And players can play with an open clubface, for example, using just about any grip—Zach Johnson has a very strong grip but aims the face open.

We prefer a slightly open attachment for our baseline draw and straight shots. However, many of the grip and clubface variations we're about to discuss could make a ball fly straight to the target if offset by alignment or wrist actions during the swing. Those adjustments aside, the square attachment is designed for hitting a straight shot, with the ball starting at the target and flying straight. Here's how you should set the three pieces of the attachment to promote a straight ball flight:

1. **Clubface.** Aimed slightly right of the target, not dead square as you might expect, to allow for the split second the ball is on the clubface as the club completes its downward arc.

2. **Butt of club.** Pointed at the top of the pants zipper. Here you're simply conforming to the design of the golf club. Holding the shaft at this angle encourages a square clubface. To picture this,

imagine you had a tee glued to the face of a lofted iron with the pointed end sticking out. If the face were square at address, the tee would point at the target. Now if you lowered the butt end of the club, setting the clubhead on its heel, the tee would point to the left. If you raised the butt end, pushing the clubhead up on its toe, the tee would point to the right. With the butt of the club at the top of your zipper (below), the tee would point straight, which means the face is square to the target.

3. **Hands**. Turned 20 to 30 degrees clockwise from vertical (right), defined as the position where the back of the left hand and the palm of the right hand face the target. This helps keep the clubface square during the swing.

To play a fade, use a closed attachment because it allows you to start the ball left of the target and curve it to the right. The closed attachment helps you guard against over-fading because you'll be swinging into impact with a closed face. Here's how to adjust the attachment elements to produce a fade:

1. **Clubface.** Aimed ten yards left of the target at address. A closed clubface tends to return closed at impact, causing the ball to start left.

2. **Butt of club.** Pointed at the middle of your zipper (below). Setting the butt end of the club a little lower than you would for a square attachment causes the face to point fractionally to the left.

3. **Hands.** Turned 30 to 40 degrees clockwise from vertical (right). This position helps you deliver the clubface at impact in a closed position, which starts the ball left, making room for a fade.

The open attachment will let you hit a draw, starting the ball right of the target and curving it left. Many elite players use an open attachment because it helps start the ball far enough to the right to prevent the ball from over-drawing. Here's how to adjust the attachment to hit a draw:

1. **Clubface.** Aimed ten yards right of the target at address. An open clubface tends to return open at impact, causing the ball to start right.

2. **Butt of club.** Pointed just above the top of your zipper, about at the belt buckle (below). Setting the handle higher at address causes the face to point fractionally to the right.

3. **Hands.** Turned 10 to 20 degrees clockwise from vertical (right). This too helps you achieve an open clubface at impact, which causes the ball to start right, making room for a draw.

Note that the closed attachment applies to the pull-fade, with contact on the front side of the circle. To hit a push-fade like Nicklaus, the kind of fade we prefer, you should use the open attachment and shift your alignment far enough to the left so you can start the ball right of your swing path and fade it to the target. This allows you to hit on the back side of the circle, taking advantage of the ball-striking and power benefits of hitting on the back side, and still move the ball left to right.

By changing the attachment, you can work the ball in different directions without changing your swing. All of the Stack & Tilt setup positions and swing mechanics described earlier apply to the fade, straight shot, and draw. Yes, there are other adjustments you can make to promote a fade or a draw, but different ball flights can be achieved simply through changes to the attachment, and this is easier than changing swing mechanics.

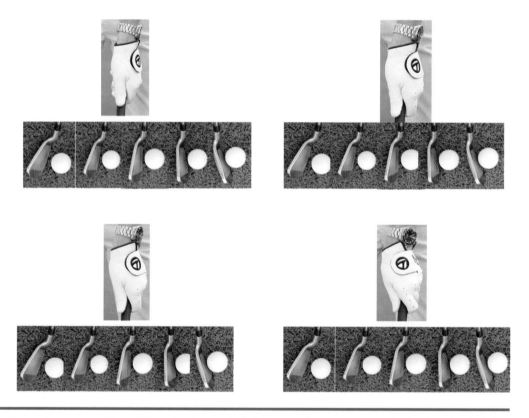

↑ **Many players combine different grips and clubface angles to produce desired shots, but the basic attachments described above are the simplest forms.**

Check your attachment against the principles outlined above. Make sure it fits the type of shot you're trying to hit—square for a straight shot, open for a draw, closed for a fade. When your ball flight strays, come back to this section to make the appropriate adjustments to regain your preferred shot pattern.

THE SHOT CONE

The historical photos in this book show that many of the principles of the Stack & Tilt Swing have already proven effective. But a quick look at the best swings in history shows that there are many ways to swing the club. There are also many different ball flights. Even our own players don't demonstrate "ideal" Stack & Tilt positions at every point in the swing. Which is fine, because it all comes down to knowing where the club is swinging and where the face is pointing at impact. A swing is effective only in that it produces a consistent shot pattern.

Every successful player has a predominant shot shape. Nicklaus and Trevino played a fade; today's best faders include Singh, Couples, and K. J. Choi. Tom Watson and Greg Norman hit a draw, as do the majority of current tour players, including Sergio Garcia, Tom Lehman, and Jim Furyk. But no matter what a player's shot looks like, the key is predictability.

Average golfers also have a ball-flight pattern. It might range from a pull to the left to a shot that slices well right of the target, but they all demonstrate a pattern. Even beginners, who hit the widest variety of shots, have consistent swing tendencies that produce a predictable set of shots. When golfers feel as if their shot pattern is completely random, they're simply not looking at it with an educated eye.

As we've discussed, every shot is a function of face angle at impact and the squareness of the face to the swing path. But the face angle relative to the target is an often-overlooked variable that separates good shots from bad. Let's quickly review. To hit a draw that starts right of the target and curves left, the face has to be open to the target at impact (to start the ball right) but closed to the swing path (to curve it left). For a fade, the face must be closed to the target at impact (to start it left) but open to the swing path (to curve it right).

Circles and Cones

Of course, there is great variation within these examples, but they constitute the basic rules of shot shape.

When we look at shot pattern with our students, we use the image of a cone. To picture this, imagine you are looking at a golf shot from the downtarget view: The ball has a starting direction, a curve in the air, and an ending location. If you drew a line along the starting direction and another line from the point of impact to the ending location, you'd have a triangular area. We call that area the shot cone, and any ball that finishes inside its borders is in the cone, or within the player's normal shot pattern.

→ **The ideal shot cone for a draw starts to the right and ends at the target.**

A narrow shot cone is good, because it indicates a close relationship between swing path and clubface—and a tight dispersion of shots. But more important than the cone's width is its predictability over time. The more consistent the starting direction and curve, whether the curve is five yards or twenty yards, the better control the player has. Many great players have favored the predictability in curve of a wide shot cone, such as Bruce Lietzke, who plays a big cut, and Tom Lehman and Kenny Perry, who hit hard-turning draws. These players have learned they can start the ball well off the target line, knowing it will curve toward the target. Plus, with that much curve-producing action in their swings, they know they won't often lose a shot in the opposite direction.

Players with the narrowest cones are often the shortest hitters. Consider this: A slightly open clubface at impact might send the ball ten yards to the right on a 200-yard drive, but at 300 yards, that fade might turn into a twenty-yard slice. So the longest hitters often hit the fewest fairways, because longer shots amplify mistakes at impact. That's how players like Corey Pavin and Fred Funk have been successful on tour: They hit their targets more often than the bombers do.

Establishing a well-defined cone is something we work on constantly with our tour players. They know that the difference between a top-10 finish and missing the cut can be a few shots that curved outside their cone. But developing a shot cone is not just for tour pros. We help all of our students read and catalog their shots so that they can start putting some organization to their ball flight.

The first step in developing a shot cone is picking a starting direction, based on which way you want to curve the ball. As we've said, initial direction is determined by the angle of the clubface at impact. For simplicity, let's say the club is tracking straight down the target line when it hits the ball: An open face will start the ball to the right of the target; a closed face will start it to the left. Next comes the curve, caused by the clubface's orientation relative to the swing path. If the face is at a 90-degree angle to the path, the ball will fly straight in the direction the face is aimed. If the face is slightly open to the path, the ball will curve to the right. To make that an effective shot, the starting direction has to be left of the target. For a shot that curves left, the face is closed to the swing path at impact, causing the ball to hook. To make that a playable shot, the initial direction must be right of the target. Amateurs tend to over-curve the ball, slicing or hooking it across the target. These over-curves typically are the most feared shots in a player's pattern.

↑ **Faders should start the ball left with a clubface slightly open to the swing path (above, left); players who draw the ball should start the ball right with a face slightly closed to the path (above, right).**

The cone you use to plan shots on the course should not include over-curves or the occasional opposite curve—the ball curving out of the cone on the side of the starting direction, i.e., a pull-hook or a push-slice. If you tried to account for over-curves or opposite curves when establishing your shot cone, you'd find it difficult to pick a starting direction and take consistent aim. Think about it: A cone that had to accommodate curves in both directions would have to start at the target, which negates the whole concept of the shot cone.

Our work with Aaron Baddeley provides a good example here. A couple of years ago, Aaron was struggling with shots that started to the right and curved farther right. He was learning the hard way that playing with the fear of a ball that curves away from the target is no way to compete on tour. We told him when he practiced and played to focus on never letting a ball curve to the right of the target. He could hit a straight push; he could hit a draw; he could even hit an

The Stack and Tilt Swing

over-draw, but not an over-fade. In time, we took away the pieces that caused the over-draw. He got to the point where he could still miss an occasional shot to the right, but it was never curving right. His new cone started to the right and ended at the target.

DEVELOPING A CONE

To build your shot cone, go to the practice tee and chart a series of shots. Record both the starting direction, relative to the target, and the curve in the air. Let's say you play a fade, but your shots tend to finish right of the target. Your solution might be as simple as shifting your alignment farther to the left to allow for more right curve. That can be a quick fix, but if your shots are curving excessively, you're likely losing significant distance because you're deflecting the ball at impact with a face that's dramatically open to the path.

The other extreme is the player who hooks the ball, who starts it well right but tends to curve it too far left. Shifting the alignment more to the right can help, but shots with that much curve are difficult to control. We did say that many good players have a wide shot cone, but those players have ample distance, even though they're deflecting the ball at impact more than we would prescribe.

By looking at your shot cone, you'll start to see how the relationship between the clubface and the swing path at impact determines initial direction and curve. The next step is identifying the causes of starting direction and face angle. As we've said, alignment is rarely the most effective adjustment. Most golfers need to work on bringing their face more toward square and their path more along the target line.

If you want to develop a draw shot cone, you need to make all your shots have some curve to the left. Take the whole range to stay within, but every ball must curve to the left. Pick a starting line to the right so that all the shots curve toward the target. The left edge of the cone is the target line, and the right edge is the starting line.

To set your starting line far enough to the right, make sure of three things: (1) the clubface is aimed as far right as you want to start the ball; (2) the ball is farther back than normal in your stance, normal being two ball-widths behind the left heel for a middle iron; and

Circles and Cones

(3) your weight is forward at address. You might try moving more onto your left foot than the 55/45 standard, say, 60/40 or even 70/30, to exaggerate the weight at first.

→ **We tell slicers to set more weight left and lean the shaft forward to facilitate hitting out at the ball instead of cutting across it.**

It's important to note that when we say move the ball farther back, the handle should stay in its baseline position relative to the body: even with the inside of the left thigh. When you move the ball back but maintain the handle position, you angle the shaft more toward the target, which promotes an in-to-out path through impact—and a shot that pushes or draws.

Once you get your setup correct (face aimed right, ball back, weight forward), hit balls keeping your weight forward and maintaining the side angles in your wrists. With your weight more on your left foot, you'll make contact with the club swinging outward. Maintaining the angle between your right arm and the shaft (face-on view) also keeps the clubhead swinging out more. These are the major pieces that help the club swing in to out and promote a draw.

← **Allen Doyle hits a push-draw by moving his weight forward aggressively and maintaining the angle between his right arm and the shaft—no rolling over of the arms through impact.**

In a short time, you'll be hitting a combination of pushes and draws. Every ball will start right, and some will draw toward the target. A push and a draw have the same starting direction, but with the draw the face is slightly closed to the swing path, producing right-to-left curve. With the push, the face is square to the path, so the ball flies straight right. If you're hitting only pushes, close the face to the path slightly by moving the ball farther back or moving more weight to your front foot.

Notice we do not recommend closing the clubface more at address. Remember, face angle determines initial direction, so closing the face makes it harder to start the ball to the right, which is what the right-to-left player needs to do. This is one adjustment that even tour players get wrong. When they want to create more draw, many of them simply shut the face at address. That produces a shot that doesn't start enough to the right and usually draws across the target. To hit an effective draw, the ball has to start right of the target, so that's where the clubface needs to be at address and again at impact.

Make sure all of your shots are starting right and curving to some degree toward the target. If you start over-drawing the ball, consider adjustments that take away some of the hook, such as a weaker grip, with the hands rotated more toward the target, or the arms staying lower on the follow-through (a higher arm position indicates the more in-to-out path of a player who hooks the ball).

As you can see, to develop a draw shot cone, you don't simply apply the standard setup and swing positions detailed in the first few chapters. Going to the other extreme and then working back toward the baseline positions is the fastest way to make changes in ball flight. If you're a slicer wanting to hit a draw, you have to get out of your slice tendencies and develop hook tendencies. Once you learn to start the ball to the right and curve it left, you can work to reduce the hook.

Remember, the key to fixing ball flight is an honest and precise assessment of where your shots are starting and how they're curving. Accuracy in diagnosing ball flight is the critical first step in correcting errors. To be an effective golfer, you have to have control over the path and face at impact. The basic form of the swing applies to any of the shots we've described; it's the same for any ball flight. The key is developing a pattern and understanding the geometry behind it.

Everybody knows golfers who have unorthodox swings but play great because they control the pattern of their shots. And everybody knows golfers who have good-looking swings but can't break 90. The details we've explained in this chapter will help you understand what makes the ball go where it goes. The correct form described earlier is the necessary starting point, but ball control is what separates great golfers from the rest.

7

PRIORITIES AND DRILLS

TOMMY ARMOUR III

I've always believed in staying over the ball. It's something I started working on with Mac O'Grady back in the mid-nineties. If you look at the best ball-strikers, you'll see that they keep their weight centered. That idea goes way back—you can find it in a book my grandfather [Tommy Armour] wrote in the 1950s, How to Play Your Best Golf All the Time.

I met Mike and Andy about ten years ago, and they've helped me keep my swing tuned up at tournaments. It's great that one of them is at every event; they can take a look and make sure my fundamentals are good. I've always tended to make a teeny sway off the ball on the backswing, so it's good to have them make sure I'm staying forward. We've also worked to keep my club on an arc on both sides of the ball.

The biggest benefits I see from the swing are better compression on the ball and less shot dispersion. I need these things because my swing is not long. There's no doubt that when you stay forward and swing the club on an arc, the ball flight is more consistent, more pre-

dictable. When you play golf shifting your weight around, how well you play depends a lot on your timing. The swing they teach is simply more efficient.

Golfers always ask us if they have to change everything they're doing to use Stack & Tilt. The answer is no. Stack & Tilt is a system of learning golf in the correct order. You don't have to do everything we teach to play well and continue getting better. If you're just starting at golf, you should build your swing from our instructions. But we realize that many people don't have the time or interest to rebuild their swings, so you can use Stack & Tilt to improve the swing you have.

This might seem to go against everything we've said so far, but we do it every day. Stack & Tilt can be used in small doses very effectively. Many swing methods do not put an order to the progression and, therefore, the whole method has to be adopted for it to work, provided it was correct in the first place. Of course, we think Stack & Tilt should be followed in its entirety, but the fact is, adding a piece or two to a player's current technique often yields great results. That's because it is a logical approach to golf: Do the most important things first, then move to the next most important, then the next, and so on. In time we hope you learn the whole swing, but in the short term, learning individual pieces will help you.

We've said that the essence of science is classification, and the science of classification is called taxonomy. Using taxonomy, we classify a player's swing to find its pattern. Understanding the pattern determines the course of progression.

Some players, through experience, are very highly adapted. Even though they might not be able to explain what they are doing, they have learned how to adapt their swings to achieve correct positions. For instance, most golfers have been taught to shift the weight to the right on the backswing. Better players have learned to compensate for this move by shifting the weight quickly to the left on the downswing. But this is an unnecessary complication: Any move off the ball multiplies the complexity of the swing.

By contrast, Stack & Tilt makes the swing as mechanically simple as it can be to reduce the degree of difficulty. Remember our example of the Olympic gymnast or diver: The higher a maneuver's degree of difficulty, the harder it is to perform without errors. The same goes for the golfer. Complexity, even if it brings the potential for great benefit, adversely affects repeatability.

As you've seen, we have instructions for every facet of the swing, but the process must be organized. Improvement can be measured one piece at a time, but the results are compounded. You should focus on the pieces that will cause the fastest, most dramatic changes. That's a matter of physics and geometry: The ball is only reacting to what the club is telling it at impact. You have to do the best you can to deliver the club to the ball to produce the shots you want, and to do it in the most repeatable way.

Through hitting good shots, you'll learn to trust yourself. Hitting bad shots creates anxiety, which comes from seeing poor results and not knowing what to do about them. So the results dictate whether or not you have to make changes. If you do, you need a plan, which eliminates the anxiety. Becoming more competent is the only way you can remove the anxiety to the point where you can play without too much thinking getting in the way.

Our goal is to educate players on the patterns that result from a certain set of swing mechanics. We do prefer that every player hit on the back side of the circle, regardless of whether he's playing a draw or a fade. A swing that moves outward to the ball at impact (hitting on the back side) creates more power and the higher loft necessary for low-lofted clubs. Ideally we want the player to push the ball to the right and draw it to the target or to aim to the left and hit a push-fade. But our system is broad enough to explain the strengths, limitations, and specifications of hitting across the ball from out to in as well.

GETTING THE PRIORITIES STRAIGHT

Everything in Stack & Tilt revolves around the fundamentals we introduced in the first chapter: (1) controlling the low point, (2) adding power, and (3) adjusting the curve. Too many golfers focus on hitting the ball longer before they develop an ability to hit it consistently, and then wonder why they don't play better. Others get caught up in shaping shots, when they don't hit the ball far enough to take advantage of any shot-making skills they have. Still others work on things like grip, posture, alignment, even swing plane, without even knowing what those elements do. The best way to improve your game is to work in a systematic way, and that's what we teach.

❯ Controlling the low point of the swing is the first measurable difference between good and poor players. It should come just after impact on iron shots.

Hitting it solid

Consistent contact is a matter of controlling the low point of the swing. To review, the axis of the swing—the shoulder center—should stay in one spot from start to finish. For the center to stay stable on the backswing, the left shoulder must turn in a circle. This conforms to the law of the circle: If the left shoulder moves in a circle, the shoulder center can stay fixed. Remember the compass you used back in geometry class, with the needle on one arm and the pencil on the other: For the pencil to trace a circle, the needle end must remain in place. Moving the axis of the swing requires a recovery move before impact to control the low point—that is, assuming you had the center in the right place at the start.

The Stack and Tilt Swing

To monitor your ball-striking ability, you also should be aware of your swing radius, which is a line from your left shoulder to the club-head. Provided your shoulder center stays in place, two factors affect the length of the swing radius: the arms and the wrists.

During the backswing the wrists hinge the club to about 90 degrees with the left arm, which shortens the radius significantly. Coming down, the wrists unhinge as a result of the arms swinging downward, and the radius gets longer. To be more precise, the downward force of your left arm pulling away from your chest and your right arm straightening unhinges the wrists, which restores the radius to its original length. The club gains velocity through the release of these arm and wrist levers.

Consider also the side angle in the right wrist (the angle between the right arm and the shaft from the face-on view). Because many golfers think they are supposed to roll the club through impact, they throw away this angle on the downswing. As we discussed earlier, the wrist angle should be set at address and remain constant throughout the swing. If the angle is increased on the downswing, the swing radius lengthens too early, putting the low point behind the ball and usually causing fat shots.

→ **Hitting punch shots is a great way to learn the basic form. Keep your weight forward, your arms straight, and the handle forward.**

Here's an exercise we teach to students to help them maintain that side angle in the right wrist. Using an 8-iron, set up to a ball and swing halfway back, focusing on holding that right-wrist angle. Then swing halfway through, keeping that angle in the wrist. Use the ground as a backboard, feeling the resistance by keeping the butt of the club forward. This is a mini-version of the full swing, with the same stable right wrist you should feel on every shot.

DRILL

Hit the ground

This is one of the first drills we use with students who have trouble taking a divot on the target side of the ball. Without a ball, simply swing the club and hit the ground, using half-swings at first. We don't care if you hit an inch or a foot behind the spot where the ball would be—the object is to identify the low point of the swing, then gain some control over it. Little by little, start moving that low point forward by shifting more weight toward the target and pushing the butt end of the club forward. It will help you to keep both arms straight through impact. With some practice, you'll consistently hit the ground in front of where the ball would be. What you're feeling is a stable right wrist, no flexing in the arms, and the weight forward, all basic rules of Stack & Tilt—and solid ball-striking.

Close your left eye

You want the ball in the center of your vision throughout the swing. If your head moves to the right, you might lose sight of the ball with your right eye. This drill helps you recognize if the ball is shifting from your central vision. Set up normally, close your left eye, and hit some balls. (Make sure your neck is down enough at address.) Seeing the ball with only your right eye, you'll quickly stop moving your head to the right or upward. This is a powerful drill, because losing sight of the ball is one of the most unsettling feelings a golfer can experience.

Hold your head in place

Set up with your head against a doorframe, or have a friend mark your head position, and simulate your backswing. If your head moves forward and downward, you're not straightening your spine or you're tilting to the left too fast. If your head moves to the right or upward, you're not tilting left enough or you're straightening your spine too fast. If your head comes off the doorframe, you're straightening your spine but you're not tilting to the left. Keeping your head in place proves you're achieving a perfect blend of tilting left and extending your spine.

Crush the can

Place an empty soda can under your left foot at address. Swing back and start your downswing by crushing the can. This downward pressure in your left leg immediately transfers more weight to your front side. In an actual swing, this leaning into your left side starts your hips moving laterally toward the target, one of the master moves of Stack & Tilt.

Straighten your right leg

Another issue we see with higher-handicappers is that they let the right knee flex too much on the downswing, causing the shoulder center to move back. The right leg should straighten on the backswing, then regain its original flex on its way to straightening again after impact. But some golfers let the right leg over-flex or push toward the left leg. To fix this fault, set your right leg straight at address with almost all your weight on your left foot. Hit some balls while keeping your right leg straight throughout the swing. Start with shorter, slower swings. You'll quickly get the feel for the weight being left, and coming down you'll keep your shoulder center forward. As you hit balls, straighten both legs through impact, pushing your belt higher. You'll see that your hips are free to keep pushing your rear end under your torso to the finish. This straightening of the legs and raising of the hips will keep the divot shallow. This is how your normal follow-through should feel.

Checkpoints for the low point

We've said that a fixed shoulder center and control over the swing radius promote solid contact, but let's look at some key swing positions that control these factors.

Spine tilt. The spine must tilt as described earlier—to the left on the backswing and to the right on the downswing—to keep the swing axis in one place. Swing in front of a full-length mirror or have a friend stand in front of you from the face-on view. Set your shoulder center over the ball at address, and then swing to the top. If your center moves to your right, you're not tilting your spine enough to the left.

Then swing to the finish, again marking the position of your center. If it shifts toward the target, you're not tilting enough to the right on your follow-through. If it shifts away from the target, you're probably over-flexing your right knee on the downswing or not getting your hands down fast enough; both moves can cause your center to move back.

Ball position. For solid contact to occur, the impact point on the swing arc (just before the low point for every club except the driver) must match up with the ball position. The baseline measurement for ball location that we use—two ball-widths behind the left heel for a middle iron—moves back for shorter clubs and forward for longer clubs. The wedges should be played in the center of the stance, and the driver in line with the left heel.

To check ball position, set up and lay a club on the ground, extending from your left heel. Make sure the ball is in the right spot in the range described above, relative to the club on the ground. Be careful if you play from an open or closed stance: For accuracy, the ball must be measured at a 90-degree angle to your stance line, not a 90-degree angle to the target line.

↑ **The angle between the right arm and the shaft should be established at address and maintained through impact, even with the driver.**

The side angle in the right wrist. As we've said, this angle should remain intact throughout the entire swing. If it increases on the downswing, the swing radius gets too long, causing the low point to move back and the club to swing across the ball. Contact becomes unpredictable and the out-to-in path causes pulls, fades, and slices. Take your setup in front of a full-length mirror and make a swing, posing the impact position. Make sure the angle between your right arm and the shaft has stayed intact.

Adding power

Once you gain control over where your swing is bottoming out, it's time to start adding power. The good news is that most amateurs have enough clubhead speed to hit the ball far enough to play well. But most of them don't optimize the ball speed off the clubface be-

The Stack and Tilt Swing

cause they don't strike the ball in the center of the face and hit with the correct loft.

Pros get the most ball speed from the clubhead speed they generate because they hit the ball solidly; amateurs mis-hit the ball and therefore waste potential power. Fat and thin hits typically go shorter distances, but even shots that seem like pure strikes but are made with an excessively open or closed clubface sacrifice yards.

Amateurs generally make too steep a descent into impact and add loft to the face, so they hit high-lofted clubs too high and low-lofted clubs too low. Better players do the opposite: They hit the shorter clubs lower than the built-in loft prescribes and the longer clubs higher, optimizing launch and ball speed in both cases.

Once the concept of hitting with positive and negative loft is understood, the various power sources that combine to create your power potential can be examined. The quickest way to increase your distance is to identify the power source that is most lacking in your swing and focus your efforts there. Here we'll look at the three main contributors to power: (1) swinging the hands on an inside path, (2) releasing the forward flex of the body, and (3) using the levers in the arms and wrists.

We've talked about the benefit of swinging on an arc versus swinging in a straight line. Your hands should not move straight back from the ball or straight through the ball. Power comes from moving your hands around your body, with your arms riding on your chest all the way back and through.

The body tilt changing on the backswing and downswing increases the body's turning capacity, which is the biggest power generator in the swing. The more your body turns on the backswing, the more speed you'll produce turning through the ball. We don't teach maximizing the differential, or stretch, between the hip and shoulder turns as a source of power the way many instructors do. Increasing your overall rotation away from the ball gives you more room to accelerate on the downswing. To do that, you have to free up your hips to turn back by straightening your right leg, because your shoulders turn only as far as your hips allow them. On the downswing, you have to release your hips from their forward tilt toward the ball so they can keep turning. That's the thrusting up of the lower body through impact.

→ Coming down, the shoulders and arms accelerate, then slow down before impact, causing the wrists to unhinge and maximize speed.

A third source of power is the release of the arm and wrist levers on the downswing. You create a certain amount of power through the body pivot—tilting and extending the spine on the backswing and downswing. But the downward and outward extension of the arms and the unhinging of the wrists amplify this power. Your left arm should pull away from your chest on the downswing, and your right arm should straighten, adding speed. These actions cause your wrists to unhinge, which also multiplies the speed. Without this powerful lever assembly working correctly, your torso is left to create all the power.

← Notice how the wrists are unhinging but the arms are not rolling over as taught in the conventional release.

Through impact, your arms and wrists have the job of rehinging the club (a mirror image of the wrist hinge on the backswing). This serves to slow down the swing after the strike, but it also optimizes the transfer of momentum to the club. Your hands actually slow down through impact, which sends speed down the shaft to the club-head (remember the image of the cracking whip). Your wrists begin to rehinge shortly after impact, and by the time your right hand reaches shoulder height, they have rehinged the full 90 degrees. Many golfers disregard this rehinging as a power source because it happens primarily after impact, but the process is under way well before that, proven by the fact that the hands slow down—the first step in rehinging.

Swing under the shaft

Have a friend stand in front of you from the face-on angle and hold a club one inch off your right shoulder at address. Now hit balls without your arms touching that club. This will ensure that your arms stay low, swinging on an arc around your body. If your arms lift and swing more vertically, they'll crash into the club. Keeping your arms low allows them to stay on a circular arc and build speed as they go.

Rehinge the wrists

The idea that you have to swing your hands and arms faster to increase speed is a myth. Just as wrist hinge on the backswing stores power, rehinging the wrists on the follow-through creates more speed at impact. For the wrists to rehinge, the hands and arms have to slow down through the hitting area. Try hitting some iron shots with a full backswing and a half-finish, with your arms stopping parallel to the ground. First, try keeping your wrists firm through impact so the club points out to the target, and see how far the ball goes. Then, swing back again and rehinge your wrists through impact so your arms finish in the same place but the club gets to vertical. You'll see you create more speed when you rehinge. Your arms have traveled the same distance but the clubhead has moved farther—and faster.

Keep your head still

Asteady head means your shoulder center is stable, which we've discussed as a key to solid contact. But it is also a power producer. Imagine you were swinging a weight on a string, like a lasso: The tighter the circle you make with your hand, the faster you can swing the weight. The same concept applies to the golf swing. Have a friend stand just outside the ball and hold the grip end of a club off your right ear as you practice making swings or hit balls. Your head should not bump into the grip. Do the same exercise with the club off your left ear to make sure your head isn't moving forward. Remember, a steady axis translates into more clubhead speed and increased precision.

Tuck the butt

To get the feel for the lower-body thrust through impact, try making half-swings, so that your left arm is parallel to the ground on the backswing and your right arm is parallel at the finish. The priorities here are: arms straight, raise the belt, tuck the butt. The shorter swings help isolate the lateral and upward movement of your lower body. Try it: You'll find it easy to make solid contact, and you'll hit the ball farther than you'd expect, illustrating that lower-body action is an essential power source.

Checkpoints for power

We've talked about how tilting and stretching the spine on the backswing and downswing frees up the body to turn more and how the arm and wrist levers multiply the speed of the body pivot. Now let's look at the swing pieces that contribute most to the production of clubhead speed and, therefore, ball speed.

Hand path and wrist angles. Your hands and arms should start the club moving immediately to the inside. By the time the club reaches parallel to the ground in the backswing, your hands should be over the ball of your right foot. From there your hands continue on their orbit around your body until they reach the top, when they are well outside your right shoulder, as viewed downtarget. Throughout the backswing, your wrists hinge continuously until they form that 90-degree angle with your left arm. When the backswing is complete, your left arm is nearly covering the line of the shoulders (downtarget view). Check this position in a mirror or on video.

→ **At the top, the hands should be four to six inches outside the right shoulder, not over the shoulder or the neck.**

The Stack and Tilt Swing

When your left arm pulls away from your chest on the down-swing, it moves the club downward fast enough to keep it well to the inside. Because your shoulders are turning toward the target, your wrist angle actually increases, which stores additional energy. But as your right arm starts to straighten, your wrists begin to unhinge. They fully unhinge through the shot and, as we've said, begin to re-hinge after impact. When your right arm parallels the ground in the follow-through, it should be angled well inside the target line, proving that the hands have stayed on the circular arc.

Body rotation. The amount of hip turn directly affects the amount of shoulder turn, so the hips are a good indicator of the body's overall range of motion. We've said that the straightening of the right leg and the stretching of the spine allow the body to turn on the backswing. Start by checking your leg action as you swing. Set up with a mirror off your right side, and as you swing to the top, make sure your right knee is nearly straight and your left knee has flexed several inches toward the ball.

Now turn so your rear end faces the mirror at address. Swing to the top and make sure your right hip is higher than your left by three or four inches. This is a better angle than face-on because the right hip is clearly in view. A higher right hip proves that your right leg has straight-ened and, therefore, your hips have made a full turn. From this view you can also see how your right leg is vertically aligned with your torso. This indicates that the forward tilt of your spine has been released; if it hadn't, your torso would be tilted to the right, outside your right leg.

➔ **When the right hip turns back high and the spine fully extends, the right leg and the upper body are aligned correctly—in a straight line.**

When your left arm reaches parallel to the ground on the way down, your shoulders should be at a 45-degree angle to the target line and your hips square. At impact, your shoulders should be parallel to the target line, with your chest facing the ball. And by the time your right arm parallels the ground after impact, both your hips and shoulders should be turned 90 degrees forward, pointing at the target.

Lower-body thrust. Remember, your hips must move laterally and then upward on the downswing. Check the lateral motion by making sure your left knee is ahead of your left ankle when you're halfway down (face-on view). Pose this position: Your knee should be two inches outside the ankle when the club is parallel to the ground, and it should continue to move farther forward as the swing progresses. Practice the downswing in slow motion in front of the mirror and be sure that your left knee is moving forward.

→ **To check that the lateral motion is sufficient, pose the halfway-down position and make sure the left knee is ahead of the left ankle.**

The Stack and Tilt Swing

As for the upward movement of your hips and the straightening of your legs, the best indicator is the height of your belt. We've said that your right hip gets higher on the backswing, but the center of your hips maintains its address height. Coming through the ball, your legs straighten and your entire pelvis rises three or four inches. Take some swings in front of the mirror and note the level of your belt buckle at address and after impact: It should rise at least a few inches. That's proof that you're pushing up with your lower body.

Controlling shot direction

Among better players, the degree and consistency of curve is the chief variable. Some good players hit the ball fairly straight, and others move it fifteen or twenty yards in the air. But remember our discussion on shot cone: A narrow cone is not necessarily better; it's the predictability of the cone that matters most. Players who are always curving the ball toward the target, even big curves, are better off than those who tend to cross the target by over-curving shots. Players who over-curve have more difficulty planning and executing shots on the course.

As discussed in the last chapter, the attachment in large part determines the angle of the clubface at impact, making it one of the primary factors in shot direction. We've also talked about ball position as it affects your ability to make solid contact, but it's also important in shot direction. With the ball position back, you'll tend to make contact on the back side of the circle, with the club swinging to the right. Ideally, the face is closed to this swing path so the ball curves to the left. With the ball forward, you'll tend to make contact on the front side of the circle, with the club swinging to the left. Then you want the face open to the path, so the ball curves right.

Alignment also plays a major role in shot direction. If you shift your stance at address to the left or right, it affects not only where on the circle you hit the ball but also the face angle to the path. Think back to our example of Nicklaus: He shifted his alignment to the left so he could hit a push-fade. His ball flight started left of the target but right of where he was aligned. With the clubface open to the path, his shots moved farther to the right. Nicklaus's technique proves that alignment is a major factor in determining not only initial direction but curve as well.

Swing to first base

Charlie Wi uses the image of a baseball diamond to check his swing path through the ball. Charlie is a great one for reciting mental cues in his head as he practices. He imagines he's standing at home plate and trying to "hit to first base." This reminds him to swing out enough to start the ball right and curve it left to the target. In truth, he wants to start the ball at the second baseman and draw it to centerfield, but even tour players need to exaggerate the feel. The function of this drill is to increase the linear force (hip slide) relative to the rotary force (torso turn). Try this "hit to first base" cue when you practice Stack & Tilt.

Pinch the tees

Keeping your upper arms against your chest throughout the swing helps your hands and arms trace a circular arc around your body. Eric Axley talked earlier about using this drill. Stick a tee under each armpit, and practice hitting balls. If the tees fall out at any point in the swing, your arms are pulling away from your chest and swinging too upright.

Miss the range basket

To provide instant feedback we often use a physical object with our students to block the way of a faulty swing path. For players fighting an out-to-in path and a slice, we sometimes lay a range basket on its side, just outside the ball with the bottom facing the player. To avoid hitting the basket, the student has to swing into the ball from the inside. Use this if you're trying to fix a slice (make shorter swings at first so you don't smash into the basket at full speed). To make it even harder, you can angle the basket toward your right foot, which should keep your swing even more to the inside. The priorities of this drill are as follows: (1) Keep your hands in on the backswing; (2) move laterally more than you turn on the downswing; and (3) keep the butt end of the club forward at impact. These elements will help you swing more in to out through the ball.

Feet together

Players who get the club trapped too far inside on the downswing often slide too fast with the lower body, which drops the hands and arms way behind them. To fix this, hit some iron shots with your feet together and focus on swinging your arms as fast as you can. From this narrow stance, your lower body won't race out of sequence, and your arms won't get stuck too far to the inside. Then go back to your normal setup and try to feel your hands swinging down faster.

Don't hit the box

This is a great one for the player who swings too severely in to out through impact. Take your address with a middle iron and have a friend place an empty box between your feet and the target line, just back of the center of your stance. Position the box so the shaft just misses it as the club swings on the proper path back and down (as a measuring point, use the hands tracking over the ball of your right foot). Now make some swings—and eventually hit some balls—without touching the box. This drill serves two purposes: First, it helps control the path of the shaft in the backswing. Any independent rotation of your arms going back will send the shaft too far to the inside and into the box. Second, it helps control the downswing path. If your problem, like most players who swing too in-to-out, is that you stand up too

fast on the downswing and the butt of the club gets too high, this drill will provide immediate feedback. The fix is to swing your hands away from your head faster coming down.

Checkpoints for curve

The first step in assessing curve is to determine whether the ball is really curving at all. Players often tell us the ball is going left or right but they don't know if it's flying straight in that direction or curving there. Worse, they think they do know and they're wrong. The causes of a pull, for instance, are totally different from those of a hook, but the ball might end up in the same spot. Keep our classification chart of the 11 possible shots (pp. 122–123) handy so you can learn to accurately read your ball flight. Check the following positions to find out what's making your shots go where they go.

Face angle. The easiest way to determine face angle is to simply see whether the ball is starting left or right of the target. Have a friend stand behind you or pick an object in the distance, like a tree or house on the horizon. As discussed earlier, we often use a long rope to represent the target line and to show precisely where a player is aimed and as a reference point for where the ball starts. Hit some shots and see if the ball is starting left or right of the object you selected. That will tell you where your face is aimed at impact.

Face relative to path. If the ball curves to the right, the face was open to the path; if it curves left, the face was closed. We'll get to ball-flight corrections in the next chapter; for now we only want you to determine where the face is pointing in relation to the path. Remember, the more you swing out to the ball, the better the chance the face will point to the left of the path. The more you swing across the ball, the better the chance the face will point to the right of the path. Therefore, swinging out makes it easier to curve the ball left, and swinging across makes it easier to curve it right.

Impact shaft angle. From your setup position, imagine the angle of the club to the ground as establishing a tilted plane (downtarget view). If the shaft gets more upright at impact, the plane is shifted to the right. If the shaft gets flatter, the plane is shifted left. Try making some swings with a mirror off your right side, posing at impact and looking at the angle of the shaft. Make sure it matches the angle you set at address.

→ **Pushing the hips forward enough helps keep the shaft at the same angle to the ground set at address.**

Our objective in this chapter has been to help you start assessing your game and putting the Stack & Tilt Swing into play. We've revisited the fundamentals—contact, power, and shot direction—because they are the priorities you should follow. Checkpoints are important tools for seeing where you stand and what you need to work on. Start with making consistent contact, then add power, then learn to control your shots. If you tackle these elements one at a time, and in this order, you'll be following a systematic approach to improving your golf swing.

FIXING COMMON FAULTS

Our goal with all of our students is to identify their biggest problems and teach them the principles that will help them recognize the pattern in their swings. On a global scale we hope to advance the game by establishing standards that give every player a road map to improvement. To do that, we need a system broad enough to include every golfer but narrow enough to measure small differences from shot to shot with highly skilled players.

You have to understand what you're working on to be able to recognize if you're succeeding in your practice. You might have multiple problems, in which case the correct progression of the practice is paramount to getting any one thing exactly right. This progression through the swing applies to players of all levels. The degree of detail for the high-handicapper and the professional won't be the same, but the principles should be. This chapter is about the common faults we see during the process of diagnosing swings. We have created "fault trees" to demonstrate the progression of a particular fault as it relates to the system as a whole.

Every golfer knows that fixing a golf swing can be complicated, and that it's easy to get bogged down. Even tour players lose sight of the forest for the trees. Only the individual player can decide, based on his grasp of the material, what is the acceptable level of detail he is ready to process, and the ball flight always tells if the information is correct. If you simply want to hit the ball solidly, you'll find satisfaction quickly. Establish your pattern by understanding the principles set forth in the previous chapters. Consistency is the most admired trait of the game's best ball-strikers. So let mechanics produce a pattern and over time feel will reproduce it.

We think of the Stack & Tilt Swing as a collection of setup and swing pieces, each with a specific purpose or effect on the ball. Sometimes adding one piece to a player's technique makes a big difference. Adding the next piece and the next increases the level of sophistication. But Stack & Tilt is a comprehensive system, which keeps you from wandering off on tangents. Diagnosing which piece to address is the most important thing a golfer can do. Based on our experience measuring golf swings, we can make recommendations to shorten the improvement process, but all golfers will face problems along the way. That's why it's critical to subscribe to an overall system: Knowing the pieces and what they do will keep you from trying to change the template as you go, something we struggled with as players.

Some golfers look at their shots and think they must be making a different mistake on every swing. That's never the case. Even novice golfers have a remarkably consistent fault pattern, if not shot pattern. Consider fat and thin shots. They seemingly occupy opposite ends of the contact spectrum, but in reality they come from the same fault: The low point of the swing is behind the ball. Fat shots occur when the club crashes into the ground before reaching the ball. Thin shots usually come from trying to prevent the club from hitting behind the ball, often by bending the arms; the player hits the ball on the upswing, after the club has already reached its low point.

← When the swing bottoms out behind the ball, the result is either fat contact or a thin shot hit on the upswing.

Confusion can also occur if you alternately hit pulls and slices, a common pattern with average golfers. The swing path cutting across the ball from out to in causes both shots. With the pull, the clubface is square to the path, so the ball flies straight left; with the slice, the face is open to the path, so the ball curves to the right. On consecutive swings, you could hit shots that end up fifty yards apart, one in the left rough, the other in the right, with a similar swing but a different face angle. If you hit pushes and hooks, on the other hand, you have the same problem in the opposite direction.

→ We track the identity of each piece of the swing so that players can assess the individual pieces when they practice.

So the same basic fault can result in dramatically different shots. This is why you have to assess a lot of shots to understand your pattern. Hit some balls, preferably with a long rope or the like stretched out along the target line as described earlier. This helps you see exactly where your body is aligned and the starting direction of the ball. With your alignment controlled, you can more easily identify what the swing or clubface is doing to affect the shot.

Ask yourself these questions:

1. Where is the ball starting? (If the long rope is used, on which side of the rope?) This tells you where the clubface is pointing at impact.

2. Which direction is the ball curving? This gives you some indication of the path of the club.

3. How many balls curve across the line (rope) and how many curve toward the line without crossing it? This provides you with a metric not just for recognizing, for example, if the face angle is open (starting direction) but the relationship of face to path (degree of curve). In this way, you can put some organization to your shot pattern. This simple diagnostic process equips you with the information you need to apply the concepts detailed in this book and start controlling your shots.

Pattern recognition combined with an understanding of the rules laid out in the preceding chapters will begin to make the diagnosis of faults simple, accurate, and systematic. The fault trees that follow are organized in order of sequence, from the setup through the swing. Once you identify the correct tree by finding your problem ball flight listed under the headings, you can start to work your way down the list of possible causes in the order presented. You might find one or more variables that you need to address. It is best to try one at a time to test the effect that each individual piece has so you can determine if you've found the right cause.

In addition to the shots covered in the classification system previously discussed, we've included in the fault trees several other mishits that don't necessarily go with a specific shot direction: fat and thin contact, shots that fly too high or too low, and shots that lack distance. As some of the most common mis-hits in the game, these shots deserve consideration in any discussion of fixing faults.

FAULT TREE NO. 1: LOW POINT BEHIND THE BALL

Mis-hits: fat and thin contact

← **The shoulder and hip centers are too far back, causing the club to hit the ground behind the ball.**

The first standard that differentiates good players from high-handicappers is where they hit the ground and how consistently they hit that spot. The heavy shot is commonly associated with a low point behind the ball, but as we've said, the thin or topped shot often results from the same fault. On these shots the low point is also too far back; the difference is that the club makes contact while swinging up from the low point. Here are the possible causes:

Fixing Common Faults

1. Weight location. The weight is not forward enough at impact. This can be a problem with the lower body or upper body. The lower-body weight (hip center) can be back too far in the setup, or can slide back during the backswing or downswing. Likewise, the upper-body weight (shoulder center) can be back too far in the setup, or can shift back during the backswing or downswing.

►**Fix:** To correctly position your weight 55/45 on the front side with the lower body, move your hips forward at address. On the backswing, straighten your right knee, allowing your hips to turn and not slide, so that your weight is 60/40 when the club reaches the top. On the downswing, move your hips laterally early enough so your weight is 90/10 at impact.

►**Fix:** To set your weight correctly with the upper body, make sure that the notch in your sternum is forward of the center of your stance at address. On the backswing, tilt your spine to the left as you turn your shoulders to keep the shoulder center in place. On the downswing, pull your left arm down and away from your chest and straighten your right arm as your hips slide toward the target. You might have to focus on straightening your right knee faster to keep your shoulder center from moving back as the club approaches the ball.

NO!

→ When the elbows pull apart, the wrists unhinge too early. Keep the elbows close together to preserve the hinge.

The Stack and Tilt Swing

2. **Wrist action.** Because of improper wrist and right-arm action, the swing can get too wide too soon on the downswing, causing the low point to move behind the ball.

►**Fixes:** Using a marker, put a dot on the heel pad of your left hand, and make sure when you take your grip that the dot is on top of the club. This seats the handle in the fingers of your left hand, which facilitates wrist hinge on the backswing. The angle between your right arm and the shaft that you establish in the setup (face-on view) should be maintained throughout the swing—remember, the side angles in the wrists stay fixed. Releasing this angle on the downswing makes the swing wider, often moving the low point back and causing deep divots.

Your wrists might hinge correctly going back but then release prematurely on the downswing due to the right arm straightening too soon and exerting an outward force on the shaft. This also moves the low point back. Make sure your right arm does not start to straighten until your left arm is parallel to the ground on the downswing; if it straightens too early, the wrists will unhinge and shift the low point behind the ball.

← Mark the heel pad of the left hand and make sure the dot is on top of the grip at address.

FAULT TREE NO. 2:
SWINGING ACROSS THE BALL

Mis-hits: pulls, over-fades, slices, too high, too low, lack of distance

↘ An out-to-in swing path leads to a pull when the face is square to that path or varying degrees of slice when the face is open to it.

This category covers all shots that start to the left and either stay left or over-curve to the right, as well as shots that start straight and curve right. If the face is square to the target at impact, the more the path moves across the ball, the more the ball will slice. This proves that swinging across the ball, even with a face that's square to the target, causes a slice. Hitting with positive loft is also a problem here, because the player often tries to add loft or to open the face to get the ball in the air. A lack of ball speed, and distance, commonly results from a glancing blow with the club sliding across the ball with an open face.

The Stack and Tilt Swing

1. **Ball position.** If the ball is too far forward in your stance, the club will tend to swing across the ball from out to in, because it has completed its outward arc and is swinging back to the inside by the time it reaches the ball.

►**Fix:** Proper ball position is a matter of maintenance. Check its position periodically, and always when you practice. Lay a club on the ground between your feet, extending to the ball at a right angle to your intended starting line. For a middle iron, make sure the ball is two ball-widths behind your left heel. For a driver, play the ball off your left heel; for wedges, midway between your heels.

2. **Weight location.** With your weight too far back, you're inclined to swing across the ball. Your weight can be too far back at address, or can move back on the backswing or downswing.

►**Fix:** Set your weight 55/45 on your front foot in the setup. The weight should move slightly to the left as you swing to the top, 60/40. Then it moves to the left evenly on the downswing as the hips slide toward the target. If your hips stop sliding but continue turning, the club tends to pull across the ball. Make sure your hips keep pushing forward through impact.

↑ When the hips stop moving forward but keep turning, the club cuts across the ball. The left photo is a draw swing, and the other two are fade swings.

↑ **Here's what happens when the hips stop sliding forward:** The club swings past the left arm, moving the path across the ball.

3. Butt of the club. When the grip end of the club is too far back at impact, the clubhead will cut across the ball. With this fault, your right wrist typically rolls over your left wrist through impact, which moves the butt end back.

►**Fix:** First, understand that your wrists should not roll through impact. This causes you to throw out the angle between your right arm and the shaft. This angle can also be compromised when any part of the body stops moving on the downswing. If your right shoulder stops turning forward or your hips stop sliding toward the target, the right wrist breaks down and the shaft overtakes the left arm.

The Stack and Tilt Swing

►**Fix:** Make sure you keep your elbows the same distance apart throughout the swing and that you don't roll the shaft going back, which opens the clubface. The farther the right elbow moves up and back on the backswing or the start of the downswing, the greater the risk of the wrists rolling over through impact and dropping the butt end of the club back. Whatever the distance between your elbows at address (usually eight to ten inches), maintain that space as you swing back and down.

◣ **If the arms get too vertical in the backswing, the club tends to swing from out to in through impact.**

4. Hand path. If your hands don't move inward enough on the backswing, your arms will tend to lift off your rib cage, increasing the chances of an out-to-in downswing. Coming down, your shoulders can open too quickly, throwing your hands away from your body and onto an outside path. Also, if your hips don't push forward enough on the downswing, the club will swing across the ball.

► **Fix:** To keep your backswing shorter and more to the inside, maintain the pressure points between your upper arms and torso and straighten your right leg, which allows your hips and, therefore, your shoulders to turn more. More rotation reduces the need for a longer arm swing. On the downswing, push your hips toward the target faster to counter your shoulders opening too fast. This will keep your left arm in and the club approaching on an inside path.

5. Leg action. When your left leg straightens too quickly on the downswing, your hips spin open and push the club to the outside and across the ball. With your hips shifting laterally toward the target, your left knee at impact should still be flexed; when we measure this, the left knee is two inches in front of the left ankle at impact.

► **Fix:** Your left knee increases its flex toward the ball on the backswing, and then more weight shifts onto your left leg as the downswing begins. Focus on maintaining that flexed position longer as the club approaches impact. Pushing up on the downswing is an important power factor, but it should not come before the hips have made a significant lateral move toward the target. Your left leg should not fully straighten until your arms are parallel to the ground on the follow-through.

→ **If the left leg straightens too soon, the hips spin open and the club cuts across the ball. Keep the flex in the left knee longer.**

As we've discussed, cutting across the ball can produce a shot that starts to the left and either stays left (pull) or curves right (fade or slice). If the face is open enough at impact, the ball might start straight, but that shot will always curve to the right. But in the mishits listed above, we've included shots that fly too high or too low and shots that lack distance. Let's look at how an out-to-in path can cause these shots.

Hitting too high might not seem like a problem, but think of a drive that balloons into the right rough or a well-struck 8-iron that falls short of the green. These shots often result from glancing impact, with the clubface sliding across the ball from the outside and the face very open to the path. When this happens, the clubface does not compress the ball efficiently, so a lot of energy is lost at impact. A player with this problem might also be hitting the ball with positive loft, which increases trajectory and decreases distance.

How can an out-to-in swing path also produce shots that fly too low? Golfers who habitually swing across the ball know they fight losing shots to the right, so some of them have found ways to square the clubface to the path—by closing the face at address, rolling the wrists through impact, staying down on the ball longer, and so on. While this might keep the ball from peeling right, closing the face takes loft off the shot. It might work fine with an 8-iron, but delofting a 3-iron or 3-wood makes it difficult to produce enough carry to use those clubs effectively.

As you can see, shots that lack distance can result from either too much or too little loft at impact. Think of the ball flight as water squirting out of a hose: If you aim the hose higher, the water goes farther but only to a point, after which the distance decreases. When the face is severely open to the path, a 5-iron might fly like a 7-iron and a driver will spin high and to the right. By contrast, taking loft off the face can produce strong short irons, but when the clubs get longer, problems arise. Try holding the green with a 3-iron that you're hitting with driver loft, or hitting a driver that's effectively 4 or 5 degrees. For these and the other reasons above, hitting across the ball is a fault that any serious golfer should work to break.

FAULT TREE NO. 3:
SWINGING TOO MUCH IN TO OUT

Mis-hits: pushes, over-draws, hooks

↑ **Players who hit excessive pushes and hooks swing the hands too vertical in the follow-through. The shaft should reappear below the left shoulder (above, right).**

The shots in this category are the mirror images of those produced by the out-to-in swing just described. Here the ball starts to the right and either stays right or over-curves to the left. If the face is square to the target at impact, the more the path pushes out to the right, the more the ball will hook. The more a player swings out to the right without opening the clubface, the more closed the face will be to the path—and the bigger the hook. If he squares the face to this extreme outward path, the ball will start right and stay there.

1. Ball position. If the ball is too far back in the stance, the club will tend to swing out to it because the clubhead has not yet completed its outward arc. Although the Stack & Tilt model prescribes impact with the club swinging outward, if the angle into the ball is too much from the inside, the ball will start too far to the right and often over-curve to the left. This would make the shot cone too wide.

> ►**Fix:** As we've said, establishing good ball position is a simple routine that requires only the discipline to monitor it. Place a club between your feet and out to the ball at a right angle to your stance line. For a middle iron, the proper ball position is two ball-widths behind your left heel.

2. Weight location. With some players the weight moves too far forward too fast on the downswing, which causes the swing path to get deep to the inside. In other cases too much weight is on the front foot at address or shifts severely forward on the backswing.

> ►**Fix:** Remember the Stack & Tilt model: Set your weight 55/45 on the front foot at address and keep it there (a slight forward shift is permissible) as you swing to the top. On the backswing, keep your hips back—don't let them move toward the target. Coming down, pull your left arm down and away from your chest to speed up the club relative to the weight transfer toward the target. This will control how far outward you swing.

← If the right leg flexes too much on the downswing, the shoulder center shifts back. Don't let the right knee kick in toward the left.

3. Butt of the club. When the grip end of the club is too forward and outward on the downswing, the club swings too much out at the ball. This is often caused by excessive side tilting to the right due to your weight transferring forward too quickly, before the club has a chance to swing down.

> ►Fix: Focus on the elbows. When your spine tilts to the right too much on the downswing, your right elbow rotates inward, closer to your left elbow, which shifts the path to the right. Keep your elbows the same distance apart that they were at address, about eight to ten inches, on the backswing and downswing.

4. Hand path. If your hands fall too far behind your body on the downswing, the club swings outward too much. Keeping the left arm in too far is often blamed for this fault, but it is not necessarily the case. If you stand up too fast on the downswing without the corresponding side tilt to the right and rotary component, the path moves more to the right. Having your left arm too far to the inside might maximize this effect, but it is not the cause. One good indicator that your hands are moving too in to out is the club position in the follow-through: From the downtarget view, if the club reappears on the other side of the body at the head or neck (instead of below the left shoulder), the hand path was too much from the inside.

> ►Fix: This is a good example of how trying to get to a position in the follow-through can effect a change in the swing before impact. Videotape your swing from the downtarget view or have a friend stand behind you and mark where the club passes through your body on the backswing and downswing. Going back, the club should pass through your body at the base of your right biceps; after impact, it should reappear on the other side at the middle to top of your left biceps.

← If the spine stays tilted toward the ball, the arms and club swing through to the inside, staying on the correct circular arc.

5. Spine tilt. If the spine tilts to the right on the backswing from the face-on view, the shoulder center moves back. From this position, novice golfers tend to hit behind the ball, but better players often shift their knees forward excessively to save the shot. This leaves them tilted too far to the right, but at least they're able to hit the ball.

►Fix: To stop the shoulder center from shifting off the ball, tilt your spine continuously to the left on the backswing. This puts you in position to swing into the ball from the inside but not too far inside. Remember, the spine tilt throughout the swing—to the left going back and the right coming down—keeps the shoulder center fixed for solid contact and the swing on a circle to ensure the proper inside path to the ball.

→ **Not tilting to the left enough and keeping the left hip high tends to push the downswing to the right.**

NO!

6. Spine extension. If the player straightens the spine too soon on the downswing, the butt of the club pulls up and the path shifts out to the right.

> ►**Fix:** On the backswing, practice moving your right hip higher than your left as you turn to the top. This will retard the early extension of the spine on the downswing.

7. Right-knee flex. Players who swing too far out to the right have a tendency to flex the right knee too much on the downswing. As the club comes down, your right knee should flex from its straight or nearly straight position at the top, but it should never flex more than it did at address. When the right knee over-flexes or kicks in toward the left knee, the right shoulder drops and shifts the swing out to the right.

►**Fix:** Try the drill described earlier for eliminating too much right-knee flex. Set your right leg straight at address and keep it straight throughout the swing. Start with shorter, slower swings. You'll quickly get the feel for a straight right leg at the top, and coming down you'll keep the shoulder center forward, where it should be. As you hit balls, straighten your left leg through impact, pushing your rear end under your torso to the finish. This is how your normal follow-through should feel.

↑ **Keeping the left knee flexed for too long keeps the hips and torso from turning and pulling the club through to the inside after impact.**

8. Left-knee flex. We've said that the left knee flexes toward the ball on the backswing and stays flexed as the club starts down and more weight moves to the left foot. But if the knee doesn't start to straighten as the club approaches impact, the hips stop turning forward. Remember, the upward thrusting of the lower body keeps the hips rotating. If the left leg remains flexed, the hips can slide but can't turn. This is too much lateral motion and not enough forward rotation, and the club gets stuck to the inside.

►**Fix:** Practice making half-swings back and through, keeping your arms straight. As you do, focus on pushing your hips toward the target on the downswing and raising the level of your belt. When your arms are parallel to the ground in the follow-through, make sure your hips are turned through 90 degrees, so your belt buckle faces the target. To do that, you have to straighten your left leg through impact.

FAULT TREE NO. 4: CLOSED CLUBFACE

Mis-hits: over-draws, hooks, too low, lack of distance

→ **The combination of turning the left hand back and closing the face at address leads to a closed face at impact.**

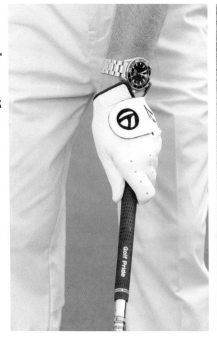

If the clubface is closed to the swing path at impact, the ball will pick up right-to-left side spin and curve to the left. If the face is closed to the target, the ball will start to the left. For players who push-draw the ball from a square stance—and that includes the majority of better golfers—shots that will not draw result from the path being not far enough to the right, rather than from the clubface not being closed enough. Remember, the biggest push-draw that does not curve across the target has the clubface significantly open to the target at impact. So the player should not try to keep closing the face to make the ball draw, unless he is intentionally hitting on the front side of the circle to hit a pull-draw.

1. Clubface aim. If the face is aimed to the left of the intended starting line at address, it will tend to return that way at impact and impart hook spin on the ball. Of course, many things can happen during the swing to change the face angle, but the first place to look is in the setup and the attachment. To hit a draw, we recommend that you open the clubface at address, pointing it at your intended starting line.

> ►**Fix:** Find a straight line, like a shaft or even a tee, and practice setting the clubface at a right angle to this line. You have to train your eyes to see the difference between open and closed. This simple exercise will make it easier for you to recognize clubface aim at address.

2. Grip/grip at impact. The relationship of the grip to the clubface can change from setup to impact, and this effect is maximized when the grip is rotated to the right, in a strong position. When a strong grip is combined with the butt of the club sitting low at address (elements of a closed attachment), the left wrist cups, or bends back. Then, if the butt of the club moves higher or more forward by impact, the clubface closes. This is because the cupped left wrist flattens, which shuts the face. This same move also can happen on the backswing if the left wrist bows or flattens as the club swings away from the ball.

> ►**Fix:** The cause of the butt of the club getting too high at impact is the player standing up too fast. To counter this, you have to slow down the rate of that upward thrust by: (1) swinging your left arm down and across your chest faster and (2) moving your hips laterally faster, which keeps the right shoulder lower and helps prevent the butt of the club from pulling up.

→ **Extending without sliding and turning the hips throws the swing path out to the right and closes the face to the path.**

NO!

3. Rate of clubface closure. Another consideration is how fast the clubface closes on the downswing. It should close uniformly to the swing arc, but sometimes the face rotates too fast. The main cause of this is the shoulder center moving back on the downswing. Look at it this way: The right shoulder must move downward, forward, and outward on the downswing, but when the shoulder center moves back, the right shoulder stops moving, which causes the clubface to close faster. This is extremely hazardous and a principle reason we advocate no shifting of the shoulder center.

> ►**Fix:** You have to make sure your shoulder center stays fixed. To do that, concentrate on two things as you swing down: (1) swinging your left arm down and across your chest and (2) straightening your right knee faster. These moves will stabilize your shoulder center and allow the clubface to close at the proper rate relative to the swing arc.
>
> Closing the clubface prematurely not only causes a hook, it can bring down the trajectory of a shot, which, as we've said, can be beneficial with shorter clubs but takes too much carry out of the longer clubs. Reducing loft is a critical element to

playing golf at a high level, but many golfers do not recognize the difference between decreasing loft and closing the face. For example, ball position and shaft lean at impact can influence the loft without changing the angle of the clubface. But for amateurs it's best to use the built-in loft on the clubface; leave those subtle shot-making adjustments to the pros.

Using these fault trees is a systematic way to identify and address your biggest problems. But the key is to evaluate a large sampling of shots, not just hit a handful of balls on the range and conclude that every swing is a new adventure. Your faults are likely to be much more consistent than you think they are. Remember, the pull and the slice, for example, might wind up fifty yards apart, but they result from the same fault: cutting across the ball. Take a good, long look at your shot pattern, and you'll find your biggest opportunity for improvement in one of these fault trees.

You might have noticed that we left two shots from our classification system out of the discussion above: the pull-hook and the push-slice. The pull-hook combines an out-to-in swing path with a closed clubface for a shot that starts left and goes farther left. The push-slice comes from an overly in-to-out path and a face so open that the ball starts right and goes farther right.

As every golfer can attest, these shots do happen, but they probably don't make up a significant portion of your shot pattern. If you hit an occasional pull-hook, you're cutting across the ball—that's the fault you need to address. Every once in a while you might shut the face so dramatically that you get it closed to the path, which is hard to do when the club is swinging out to in (if the club swings 20 degrees across the ball, the face has to be closed more than 20 degrees to produce curve to the left). That's an aberration, so despite how unplayable that shot may be, it does not mean you should focus on fixing a closed clubface.

If you on rare occasions hit a push-slice, you're swinging from too far inside—that's the fault you need to address. The open face that's causing the ball to also slice is not an issue you should pursue, unless it becomes a persistent problem. As long as the pull-hook and push-slice are rarities, they should not drive your swing-improvement plan.

To use the fault trees effectively, track your ball flight over several rounds or range sessions and look for your pattern, or shot cone. Once you know it, see which fault tree above covers your common mis-hits. You'll see just how consistent your swing faults are, and best of all, you'll have a clear direction for getting rid of them. When you take the mystery out of your mistakes, you unlock the door to getting better.

TRACKING PROGRESS

The secret to using any system of golf instruction effectively is knowing what you want to get out of it. Some golfers simply want to play without embarrassing themselves, to learn to hit the ball solidly and advance it in the right general direction. This stage usually doesn't last very long. Soon they want to improve their scores, so they need to learn to reach greens in regulation and start making more pars. Better players want more birdie opportunities, so they need to control shot shape and distance to hit different targets on command.

You have to ask yourself where you stand and where you want your game to go. With the lessons in this book, we've tried to give you a blueprint to evaluate your swing and isolate your faults, and then help you recognize the changes necessary to achieve your goals. You have to attack this process in a systematic way. Too often we see golfers trying different tips and methods every time out, hoping something will magically make a difference. There is no magic in our system or any other.

As we said early on, there are two ways to use Stack & Tilt: You can either jump in and start rebuilding your golf swing, or you can attack your faults by applying the appropriate pieces of Stack & Tilt one by one. Either way, get a taste for the swing by trying out the basic moves discussed in Chapter 2. We think you'll be inspired by the results and want to continue. Then you can pick the better route for you—rebuilding or addressing your faults. Whichever path you choose, you need to understand Stack & Tilt, so study Chapters 3 and 4.

Let's assume for a moment that you want to refine your current swing using the principles of Stack & Tilt. It's a three-step process that pulls from several of the preceding sections: (1) identify your common mis-hits; (2) pick the fault tree that covers these shots; and (3) apply the corresponding corrections. Here's a closer look.

First, identify your bad shots—where they start and in which direction they curve. For example, it's not enough to say your drives are going right: Are they starting left and slicing or are they flying straight right? The causes of those two shots are vastly different, almost opposite. Precision in reading ball flight is critical; a sloppy evaluation can start you working on things that don't address your faults. To ensure accurate analysis, refer back to the shot-classification system we laid out in Chapter 6.

Second, pick the appropriate fault tree from Chapter 8. Under each tree we listed the mis-hits it addresses. Remember, when using the fault trees, you should focus on the shots you hit most often—rare miscues, no matter how bad, should not influence your selection.

Third, apply the pieces of Stack & Tilt prescribed under each fault tree. We've organized these pieces in priority order, based on what we've seen work for students over the years. Start with the first correction and move down the list until you find the piece that makes the biggest difference in your shots. Eventually the light will go on. We see this happen every day, and it will happen for you.

Let's put an example to this. Say you tend to hit behind the ball, catching it fat or hitting it thin on the upswing, and fight a slice when you do hit it solid. We know from our discussion on fundamentals that your first priority must be to learn to control the low point of your swing for solid contact. This is Fault Tree No. 1. You must start at the top of the list of possible fixes and work your way down until you start making consistent contact.

Once you adequately address your contact issue, you can move on to your other problem: slicing. This brings you to Fault Tree No. 2: cutting across the ball. Just as you did for your low-point problem, you need to start at the top of the tree and eliminate each possible cause—ball position, butt of the club, weight location, and so on—until you see your slice improve dramatically.

This might sound like an elaborate process, but the way we've organized it makes it simple. No longer do you have to experiment with different swing fixes, not knowing if they'll have a lasting effect. Once you pinpoint your problems and find the right correction, you can focus your work in one area. Then you can spend your practice time effectively and see permanent improvement.

When we ask golfers what they're working on, we often get blank stares or, even worse, a laundry list of swing mechanics. This isn't surprising, because most golfers don't know how to filter all the advice they hear. Something might help for a few swings or a few rounds, but when it stops working, they abandon it. They don't know why it helped in the first place, so they have no commitment to it. There is no substitute for the confidence you get from knowing cause and effect.

That's not to say that you need to work on one thing for the rest of your golfing career. To the contrary, you need to prioritize your problems and address them one at a time. Keep in mind our fundamentals: contact, power, shot direction. You should advance through the instruction we've provided in that order. Trying to add distance, for example, or working on curve before you can control the pieces that produce consistent contact will only slow your improvement.

LEARN FROM PICTURES

The best way we know to monitor progress is to take pictures of the setup and swing throughout the process. We never give a lesson without our video cameras. We take individual video frames of our players and compare them to pictures showing the ideal positions in that part of the swing. We believe that most people are visual learners, and nothing beats seeing what an adjustment looks like.

Looking at pictures is also the quickest way to work through the checklists of moves and positions we've been talking about. If you have a low-point problem, for instance, you can record a few swings, study the images, and start to eliminate faults: The weight is forward, check; spine is tilting left on the backswing, check; and so on. Eventually you'll find the culprit. Without pictures, you're relying on the teacher's eye or the player's feel—both of which can and will deceive you. Even studying a single picture can be misleading; you have to hold it up to something you know is correct.

If you choose to use video, here are some guidelines we've developed:

►Set the camera square to the view you want to capture. From face-on, shoot at a 90-degree angle to the intended starting direction of the shot. For downtarget, shoot down the stance line.

→ For face-on images, always position the camera perpendicular to your starting line.

The Stack and Tilt Swing

► **Be consistent from one session to the next.** It's important to have a good frame of reference to evaluate the swing as it changes. Make sure you're using a consistent perspective and looking at the same swing position as last time.

► **Shoot at chest level.** The sternum is the center of the swing, so that's the ideal height for the camera. Filming from a squatting position or at eye level can distort the angles we've prescribed throughout the book.

↑ Video is a great learning aid, but you must be precise and consistent. Set the camera at chest height, because the sternum is the center of the swing.

► **Record several swings.** Even beginners' swings, if not their shots, are remarkably consistent, so identify the pattern and pick the swings that best demonstrate it. Disregard the occasional swing that doesn't represent the norm.

► **Focus on a single piece at a time.** One argument against using video is that you can get fixated on things other than what you set out to examine. For instance, you might not like your posture or the length of your backswing and as a result attempt to change it. To avoid this, be disciplined about focusing your work in one area, and leave the rest for future sessions.

► **Measure the movement.** You don't need a sophisticated video system with on-screen graphics or drawing tools to monitor what's happening during the swing. We use our fingers or a straight edge, like a dollar bill, to track movement or check vertical and horizontal lines.

► **Chart your progress.** Storing sample swings from each session will allow you to chronicle a swing change over time. You'll have a recorded history that you can return to if trouble comes back in a given area.

WORKING WITH THE PROS

Video has been an indispensable tool for us in working with tour players, because the changes they're making become progressively smaller and harder to measure at full speed. Plus, we're often asking them to try things that contradict much of what they've been taught throughout their careers. It's one thing to tell a player why he needs to reverse his thinking on a certain part of the swing, but it's much more powerful to show him what his swing looks like when he hits the shot he wants to hit.

It's often said that some tour pros play by feel and others are more mechanical. When it comes down to it, every tour player relies on feel. This is where video becomes critical. When one of our players views his progress with a particular piece of Stack & Tilt, he's starting to develop a picture in his mind's eye of what the correct movement looks like. In time he translates that picture into a feel, and that's what he takes to the course. Ultimately all golfers use feel, but the feel must represent the correct geometry.

We'd like to share with you, from our video archives, the changes that a few of our tour players have been able to make with the help of pictures. We've taken a ton of video, both on the driving range and during practice rounds, of these players. They've gotten so good at analyzing video of their swings that they can spot the problem and make the adjustment often without our saying a word.

Here we look at three players we've helped—Mike Weir, Charlie Wi, and Eric Axley—and track their progress with one specific piece of Stack & Tilt. These images show what they were doing when we started working with them and the improvement they made over time, shown from left to right.

Spine Angle

The first time we talked to Mike about his golf swing, he asked us why he was "drifting off the ball" on his backswing. It was the day before a tournament round—not exactly the time to introduce a major swing concept. But Mike really wanted to know, so we told him.

His spine was angled away from the target at address, and as he swung to the top, it tipped farther and farther back. This caused him to swing too much from the inside on the downswing, so he hit a lot of pushes and over-draws. Sometimes he'd fight to get the club more on line, which often made him swing the club across the ball and hit weak slices. He also had contact issues, sometimes hitting fat and thin, because his shoulder center was shifting behind the ball.

Mike needed to set up more on top of the ball, with his spine vertical, and tilt toward the target on his backswing. He needed to turn his lead shoulder down instead of inward and across his chest. When he tried this, he felt as if his head was going forward on the backswing, which was exactly what he needed to feel. In reality, by tilting toward the target he was staying centered.

To avoid actually tilting toward the target, he had to straighten his spine out of its forward tilt. That was the easy part for Mike; the hard part was tilting enough to his right as he swung back. For a while he was exaggerating this tilt in his practice swings, turning his lead shoulder down to feel like he was dipping toward the ball. This helped preset his spine in a more centered position and keep it there during the backswing. Mike increased his average driving distance by a whopping nine yards with Stack & Tilt.

Hand Path

When we met Charlie he was doing everything he thought he was supposed to do to hit the ball long and straight. He was extending the club straight away from the ball and lifting his arms off his chest onto a more vertical plane. He was keeping his right knee flexed and turning his hips level.

As a result of these moves, Charlie was swinging down steeply and cutting across the ball. He hit a lot of slices and had trouble hitting his long clubs high enough because he was taking so much loft off the face with that steep descent. To get more loft, he would try to open the face, but the more he did that, the more he would lose the ball to the right.

Our first step with Charlie was to have him straighten his right leg in the backswing, which made his hips turn more and got his hands moving more to the inside. This kept his arms on his chest during the backswing, with his hands staying lower and deeper instead of moving up and over his right shoulder.

In 2005, Charlie ranked 115th on tour in driving accuracy; today he's in the top 50. And he has even gained distance. He just needed to unlearn the things—extension, high hands, level hips—that were supposed to give him more distance and accuracy.

Hip Slide

Eric had the classic finish position when we started working with him: His upper body was tilted forward, with his head in front of his front foot. As a lot of players do, he thought this indicated a full release of the body toward the target.

Like Charlie, Eric was swinging down steeply and cutting across the ball, hitting pulls and slices. Eric is a great athlete, with a fast lower body, so he would turn his hips out of the way on the downswing without moving them toward the target enough. This would throw the club to the outside and cause the steep, out-to-in swing he was fighting.

For starters, he had to learn to slide his hips laterally on the downswing, adding more linear movement to the fast rotary action he already had. We had him practice making half-swings pushing his hips forward and not spinning them open at all. To keep his head back, we held the grip end of a club just in front of his head at address and had him hit balls without bumping into the club.

Eric quickly learned to make the correct lateral motion on the downswing, and this kept the club to the inside longer for a better delivery at impact. When he combined that move with keeping his head in place, his spine tilted away from the target at the finish—the opposite of where it was when we started with him.

WORKING WITH AMATEURS

Our process with amateur players is the same as it is for tour professionals. We videotape their swings during every lesson and compare their positions to where they were the last time. Then we add pieces of Stack & Tilt that take away faults affecting impact. We don't try to make their swings mechanically or aesthetically perfect; we try to help them isolate and adjust the positions that are getting them in trouble.

The challenge with helping amateurs is that many of them have multiple problems in their swings. That's when having a systematic approach really pays off. We're not throwing darts at the wall and seeing which ones sticks. We start with our three fundamentals, and work through them in order. Then we go to the fault trees and progress through the corrections until we find a problem. When there are multiple problems, we attack them in the sequence discussed under the fault trees.

Yes, it takes time and patience. But the system we've developed guarantees that you're always working toward something that will help in the short and long terms. As our fault trees show, there are many ways to attack the same problem, so you should move deliberately from solution to solution until you see results. Be sure to give each correction a fair trial, but if you don't see improvement, move on.

PLAYING WITH STACK & TILT

It takes a certain amount of courage to trust new swing mechanics on the golf course. Making swing changes on the practice tee is an entirely different task from putting them in play when you have to negotiate trees, hazards, forced carries, and such. You have to be disciplined enough to not let the distractions on the golf course make you second-guess what you know works.

But one great benefit of Stack & Tilt is that it should get you hitting the ball better right from the start. For example, the simple concept of controlling your swing centers will help you deliver the club to the ball more consistently. Once you can do that, you can start taking advantage of the power you're creating, and you can start regulating the distance and shape of all your shots.

When you play, keep track of your shots. Are you mis-hitting a lot of balls, or is direction your bigger problem? Are you missing left or right, and with big curves or straight pushes or pulls? Do you need more power to reach your targets? Try to get a sense of what you need the most. Recording your errant shots during a round will give you the data you need to analyze your game. While there's no replacement for working on the practice tee, the information you can gather when you play will let you capture a true picture of your game.

→ **Record your mis-hits on the course—not just where the ball went, but how it got there. Then you'll know what to work on in practice.**

The Stack and Tilt Swing

Many of our tour players have become detailed record keepers. They'll tell us after they play that they hit, for instance, three over-draws during the round, or that they hit three shots outside their cone. Sometimes they already know why, but knowing how often and how much reveals a pattern. Having a feel for how you're hitting the ball is never as real as having the facts. We've trained our students to identify more than "good shot" and "bad shot." So use those extra boxes on your scorecard to keep track of your misses. That information will drive your practice sessions.

WORKING ON THE PRACTICE TEE

If you follow the recommendations in this book, your practice sessions will never be the same. You'll have identified your shot pattern, discovered your worst miss, picked the fault tree that pertains to you, and found the correction you need to make. Then it's just a matter of working on the drills or adjustments prescribed. You'll have a simple plan to follow.

Try to avoid the temptation to jump from correction to correction. If you start seeing a different kind of mis-hit, don't assume you have a whole new set of problems. Every player has one or two swing characteristics that need the most attention. Even tour players keep working on the same things. The point is, once you figure out where your swing needs work, you have to be disciplined enough to stick with it. Sure, in time you might work on gaining distance or refining your shot cone, but you'll probably always go back to your swing tendencies. That doesn't mean you're not making progress; it means you've identified a pattern and you're addressing it. Most players never get to this point. They toil away aimlessly, trying tips or advice that may or may not apply to them.

Every golfer should use two of the drills we've discussed as part of their regular practice sessions: (1) hitting a line on the ground and (2) practicing with half-swings. Solid contact is a prerequisite for everything else, so go back to the line drill often to make sure you're in control of your low point. This is a simple drill, but it's important to check that you can do it. Grab a middle iron and make sure you can hit that line. If you can't, go back to the possible reasons why.

→ **Using the line drill, all expert players can demonstrate this consistent low-point pattern.**

Making half-swings is the second universal drill because it simplifies the motion. Whether you're working on the spine tilt in your backswing, keeping the hand path in, standing up on the downswing, or any other move, you need to see how it affects impact. Because it's easier to hit the ball with a shorter swing, practicing like this can help you isolate the correction and see if it's working.

← **Practicing with half-swings will help you pinpoint faults at impact and make corrections.**

We hope we've taught you the basics of cause and effect in the golf swing, because using them will help you improve the fastest—and make lasting changes. No golfer can truly commit to swing changes without an intellectual understanding of why he's making them. There are times when every golfer doubts what he's working on, and that's when cause and effect is critical. It's not about trust; it's about understanding.

CONCLUSION

I n the 1968 Olympic Games in Mexico City, a student-athlete from Oregon State named Dick Fosbury won the gold medal in the high jump using a new technique: He went over the bar backward—and shattered the Olympic record. The "Fosbury Flop," as his method became known, revolutionized the sport. At the Munich Games in 1972 more than two-thirds of the high-jump competitors went over the bar just like Fosbury had four years earlier.

We remind you of this historic feat because it demonstrates two points. First, the sport of high jumping had room for improvement. The leading techniques of the day were more about convention than invention. Second, Fosbury found a better way. He figured out how to create more thrust and to arch his body over the bar in a more efficient manner.

These points describe how we feel about golf. Players of all skill levels are grinding away at swings that can take them only so far. The bar in golf, so to speak, should be much higher. With better technique, the sport can and will move forward.

Golf is ready for a revolution—actually, it's more like an evolution, because the game's previous generations have given us some critical information. If you've checked out the archival images included in this book, you've seen that some of the great players from the past made the moves we teach. Whether it was Sam Snead straightening his right leg on the backswing or Gary Player standing up through impact, you don't have to look far to find the origins of Stack & Tilt.

But it's not only the swings of the past. We've had some of our players relate their experiences in these pages, but consider some other top professionals who exhibit the moves and positions in our model. Take Sergio Garcia, widely considered to be one of the best ball-strikers and straightest long drivers in the game today. Sergio swings his arms on the circular arc we've been talking about, instead of high and off the chest as conventional theory teaches. This gives him tremendous power and wonderful descending contact with his irons.

→ **Sergio Garcia shows the kind of inward hand path that distinguishes Stack & Tilt.**

Then there's Colin Montgomerie, one of the most accurate drivers in the modern era. Monty's spine actually tilts toward the target at the top of his backswing—an even more dramatic extension than we teach in Stack & Tilt. This allows him to stay over the ball and store a tremendous amount of energy in his torso. He delivers the club so accurately at impact that he rarely misses a tee shot—or a fairway.

Jim Furyk is another great example of staying centered throughout the swing. He might have an unusual looping motion, but his vertical spine on the backswing (face-on view) puts him in position to make consistent contact time after time. Plus, Jim has a huge lateral hip slide on the downswing, which prevents him from swinging across the ball and slicing. Whatever his swing may lack in aesthetics, it more than makes up for in efficiency.

→ **Jim Furyk, one of the tour's most consistent ball-strikers, makes a big hip slide on the downswing—another major element of Stack & Tilt.**

These three players are often cited as exceptions to the rules of modern technique. But why is that? They are three of the most consistent, accurate players of the last decade, and yet people dismiss their swings as unusual. We say the opposite: They have discovered, despite conventional teaching, how to hit ball after ball down the fairway and onto the green. Their swings work for good reason, and if you look for it, you'll see a lot of Stack & Tilt in what they do.

↑ **Stack & Tilt or sway back and lunge through: You decide which will make you a more consistent golfer.**

But it goes much further than that. Take it from two guys who spend thirty weeks a year on the PGA Tour: We see changes happening on a large scale. We don't see nearly as many players making a big shift off the ball on the backswing as we did five years ago. We see shorter, lower backswings and straighter arms and less wraparound in the follow-throughs. We're not saying we're responsible for these changes, but they are happening. Better, more efficient technique is taking hold.

We hope, as history has shown, that average golfers follow these trends on tour. Equipment standards have maxed out and the golf ball is probably as long as it will ever be, so the golf industry needs to turn to instruction for game improvement. The first step, as we've been discussing, is to address the golf swing in a systematic way, starting with the moves and positions that produce solid, repeatable contact with the ball. Then power and control can follow suit.

We've been fortunate that more than twenty tour players have committed to taking the leap from traditional instruction to Stack & Tilt. But bigger opportunities for improvement exist with average golfers. Think about it: Tour players are already hitting the ball solidly and far enough to play any course; they just need more control. The recreational player can benefit even more from our model, because he needs ball-striking consistency. That's where Stack & Tilt starts.

But it's not enough to learn how to hit the ball solidly or long or straight. You have to know why those things are happening. We've seen dozens of juniors who instinctively develop much more quickly than their peers, becoming top players with very little instruction. But when their swings break down, they're lost. They fall off the map, because they didn't know what they were doing right or how to get it back. They never understood the cause and effect at work in the golf swing.

Our point is, the geometry of the swing is irrefutable. The ball is only reacting to what the club is telling it at impact. That's why it's silly when a teacher says, "I don't teach a method. I work with what the player has." So do we, but we try to move every player in the same direction, toward the same ideals. Golf can be approached as a game of individual style or of geometry, but we guarantee you that geometry will win out in the end.

Here's one last story from our work on tour. In the summer of 2006, three of our players—Dean Wilson, Will MacKenzie, and Eric Axley—won their first tour events, and we weren't there for any of them. The reason is simple: They knew what they were doing. We'd worked with them during the early part of those weeks and many others. They knew the principles of Stack & Tilt, and each had a short list of priorities he needed to focus on. They got the job done in those events because they knew what was behind their good and bad shots. Every golfer needs to work toward this level of self-sufficiency. Yes, good instruction is critical, but until golf is played with a teacher in tow, the answers must come from the player's own understanding.

All golfers can and should get to that point with their golf swings. We hope this book will start you on your way.

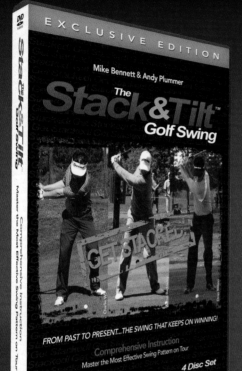